Ashe vs Connors

Ashe vs Connors

Wimbledon 1975: Tennis That Went Beyond Centre Court

By Peter Bodo

Aurum
Press

For the patrons and staff of the
International Tennis Hall of Fame at Newport, Rhode Island.
For they are the keepers of the flame.

First published in Great Britain
2015 by Aurum Press Ltd
74—77 White Lion Street
Islington
London N1 9PF
www.aurumpress.co.uk

A catalogue record for this book is available from the British Library.

ISBN 978 1 78131 395 4
eBook ISBN 978 1 78131 396 1

1 3 5 7 9 10 8 6 4 2
2015 2017 2019 2018 2016

Typeset in Spectrum MT by SX Composing DTP, Rayleigh, Essex
Printed by CPI Group (UK) Ltd, Croydon, CR0 4YY

Contents

Prologue

It is 1.54 p.m. on a still, balmy, slightly overcast day in the London suburb of Wimbledon SW19, perfect for tennis. Inside the ivy-clad walls of the Centre Court of the All England Lawn Tennis and Croquet Club, spectators chat, fidget and occasionally glance at their watches, or at the rectangular scoreboard that is blank but for two names: J. S. Connors on the top, A. R. Ashe on the bottom. Parties with a personal interest in what they are about to witness idly examine a program, or roll it up and anxiously tap it on a knee, for the smartphone is still a distant and outlandish dream. The program reminds its owner that the men's final will begin 'At 2 p.m. precisely'. When Wimbledon says 'precisely', it means exactly that.

Inside the stadium, at court level beneath the Royal Box where the Duke and Duchess of Kent are already seated, Ashe, Connors and attendant Peter Morgan wait silently for the all-clear to enter Centre Court. They're inside an airless room that is eight feet square, and has five wicker chairs against one wall, a picture of three-time 'ladies' singles champion' Maureen Connolly holding one of her trophies, and a desk and chair. The room also contains a television set, particularly welcome to the players because it gives them something to look at, helping to alleviate the tension and silence. Ashe, who will be thirty-two a few days after the tournament ends, glances at the desk; perhaps he is tempted to sit down and indulge in one of his favorite pastimes, letter-writing. But there is no time for that now.

Connors, twitchy as always, wishes they could just go out there and get on with it. He's young – at twenty-two, nine years Ashe's junior – and by nature far more impetuous. He's also confident. He's taken the measure of Ashe in the three professional matches they've played so far. Each of those was a fierce struggle that went the maximum distance in sets.

It's almost time. Ashe and Connors, still lost in their own thoughts and oblivious of each other, stand with Morgan close by the door leading to Centre Court. The door is famous in its own right for the lines that some jolly good sport from ages long past chose to have painted on a sign above the portal. It's a quotation from

Rudyard Kipling's famous poem, 'If', verse that summed up an ethos born of the ups and downs of empire building, and served as the foundation for the British notion of sportsmanship:

> If you can meet with Triumph and Disaster
> And treat those two impostors just the same.

Like Kipling, Ashe and Connors were both sent away from home by their parents at relatively young ages. Now they were young men, and probably happier on the whole than Kipling had ended up. When the attendant receives the signal that it's time, Ashe and Connors walk out through the door together. A pale blue lightbulb shines in the short hallway, alerting the players to the presence of royalty. It means they will have to pause on their way out to their chairs, turn, and bow to the Royal Box. It isn't a ritual those outside of monarchical rule are particularly fond of, thus their bow is often more of a curt nod.

Leo Turner, yet another attendant, will follow both players, carrying their bags, as they enter Centre Court and take the long short walk to their respective chairs. This is considerate; a civilized Wimbledon touch. But it also denies the men a comfortable distraction. It's as if they're being led out into the Colosseum in Rome, stripped of all they own and wearing not much more than those unfortunate sacrificial lambs once wore. Neither Ashe nor Connors can resist scanning the scene covertly, without looking at anything in particular. From which portal will the lion leap out?

A spectator laying eyes on these tennis gladiators for the first time could be forgiven for thinking that both of them needed a good meal. Connors, his face a picture in a frame of lank, chestnut hair worn Prince Valiant fashion, weighs barely 11 stone (155 pounds, or 70 kilograms) and stands 178 cm (5 foot, 10 inches). Many top tennis players have broad shoulders and pinched waists, but not Connors. His shoulders are narrow and slopping, his chest nearly concave. He is spidery, with long, thin arms (although the left, his racquet arm, is noticeably larger than the right) with the fingers of a pianist. His legs are surprisingly slender, and he wears his socks the way some children do, pulled up high and tight, halfway to his knees.

At 185 cm (6 foot, 1 inch) Ashe is considerably taller than Connors, an effect that is exaggerated by the three or four inches that his modest afro hair-do adds to his height. He's as lean as a whippet and his straight-up bearing acknowledges his military service. Where Connors has a rolling gait and swings his shoulders as if he were barging through a gaggle of slackers hell-bent on getting to something important, Ashe is light on his feet, his short, dainty steps leaving the impression that he's walking on a cushion of air.

Almost everything about Ashe suggests restraint and discipline, and this includes his warm-up jacket, a long-sleeved navy-blue number with red and white trim, with the letters USA emblazoned on the front. It's a jacket given to the Davis Cup team members, and it implies in the wearer – correctly, in this case – a measure of patriotism. Ashe is dedicated to the Davis Cup, so much so that he's been uncharacteristically outspoken about Connors' indifference to the international, nations-based team competition, an apathy that stands in marked contrast to Connors' zest for playing the role of 'heavyweight champion' in lucrative, one-off exhibition matches against other top players.

The criticism certainly rankled with Connors, so much so that just days before the start of this Wimbledon fortnight Connors' manager, a happy-go-lucky maverick named Bill Riordan, filed a $3 million defamation lawsuit against Ashe for daring to question Connors' patriotism. Ashe mischievously decided to wear the Davis Cup warm-up jacket on this finals day, and Connors himself can't be overly pleased when he sees it. His own warm-up attire is by the high-end Italian designer Sergio Tacchini (himself a former tennis player). Regrettably, it is white with red and green trim, the colors of the Italian flag.

The contrast between the two young men doesn't end there; it begins to unfurl and keeps rolling. Ashe is one of the last 'gentlemen' left in tennis, a man the eminent sociologist E. Digby Baltzell would one day describe as a 'Virginia Gentleman'. A scholar, soldier and team-mate, Ashe stands on one side of a vanishing chasm beneath which the past and future of tennis grind and push against each other like tectonic plates. On the other side of the gulf is Connors, one of the first 'showmen' spawned by the advent of Open tennis (in 1968, the lords of tennis abolished the separation of the game into pro and amateur divisions, thus helping launch a 'tennis boom'). Connors believes it is his world now, and the record he has accumulated in just a few years as a pro suggests that he is right.

Ashe is often described, even by close friends, as 'aloof' or 'remote'. He strikes some as cold, but no one questions that he strives to do what is right and appropriate, relying on reason and a fundamental urge, manifested in numerous ways, to reconcile rather than upend. Connors is emotional and 'impulsive'. He prides himself on his role as a rebel and hellion bent on conquering what some see as a stuffy, elitist tennis establishment and bending it to the will of an emerging mercantile sensibility for which the ultimate value of the game is its suitability as show business.

Physically, Ashe is a man who appears to be all sharp angles (his game has a comparable measure of slashing severity) yet inside he's composed of heartbreakingly modulated curves. It may help explain why at one point he thought he might become an architect. In Connors, what you see is what you get – a superb tennis player who freely tells one and all that he is who he is, and without apology. Ashe has a deep desire to meet Nelson

Mandela; Connors has an equally powerful urge to meet Dean Martin. Ashe will be best known for his statement (which cannot be attributed to any one person): 'From what we get, we can make a living; what we give, however, makes a life.' Connors' most famous quote will probably be 'If the sun rose and set on Wimbledon, a lot of guys wouldn't have a suntan.'

Ashe is the activist president of the ATP (Association of Tennis Professionals, the players' union that eventually became the pro tour). Connors is a dissident who refused to join the players' union and, in a different lawsuit from the one already mentioned, is suing Ashe and the ATP for $10 million. The reason? Connors was banned from playing in the French Open in 1972 because he had signed a contract to compete for the Baltimore Banners in the upstart World TeamTennis league.

Ashe is a prolific reader; Connors brags that he has never read a book and has no plans to do so. Ashe, a man ever conscious that, like it or not, he represents an entire race, sometimes wishes he could be Connors – free to say or do what he damned well pleases, free to be aggressively oblivious to public opinion. Connors never wanted to be Ashe, nor anything that comes with it.

Yet for all these unbridgeable and sometimes comical contrasts, there were many similarities between the men as well – convergences or shared experiences or tastes that might make you think that the awful truth is that, as different as we may appear from one another, we can't ever escape how fundamentally alike we are, or the limited nature of our options.

Connors takes enormous pride in describing himself as an 'outsider', which he indulges with a frequency unsated even after he retires and chooses the word as the title of his autobiography. Yet while his family was not to the country club born, it was steeped in more than three generations in tennis and is a de facto part of the tennis establishment. Ashe is the true outlier, and in a far more profound and obvious way. His father did not know one end of a tennis racquet from another, and his son sprang from an environment in which tennis was seen as a baffling, exotic pastime reserved almost exclusively for 'white folks'.

Each man carries a talisman of the future of tennis in his hand: Connors uses a Wilson T-2000 racquet made of chromed steel and introduced in 1967, while Ashe swings the Head Arthur Ashe Comp 2 model first introduced in 1969.

Each man was raised by one parent. Ashe lost his mother, Mattie Cordell Cunningham Ashe, to a toxemic pregnancy when she was twenty-seven years old; he was just seven. Some believe that his phlegmatic nature was shaped partly by that experience. The role of Gloria Connors in the life of her second son, James Scott, is a more straightforward and well-known matter. There was nothing big about 'Big Jim' Connors' role in his son's life. Gloria shaped his game, remained his primary coach.

Both Ashe and Connors represent a curious marriage of the seemingly frail with the aggressive and audacious. Neither man is a specimen, but that hidden, daring quality comes flying out at you the moment they begin to play. Ashe is often described as a 'slasher'. He lives to hit the daring, unexpected winner, often with his most fully realized stroke, the backhand. But where Ashe likes to play points that come to a boil and end quickly, Connors revels in gamboling about on the grass, lunging, diving, stretching, leaping as if he longed to be a Russian ballet dancer. In different ways, each man is a showboat.

Each man had been sent to, and developed by, a tennis guru. In Ashe's case, it was the African-American physician and tennis aficionado Dr Robert Walter Johnson. Connors was shipped off by his mother to Los Angeles in 1968, where he was tucked under the wing of the brilliant former pro and *éminence grise* of the flourishing southern California tennis scene, Pancho Segura.

Both men are devoted habitués of London's Playboy Club. This might strike some as uncharacteristic of Ashe, less so of Connors. But, then, these men are first and foremost world-class athletes. They aren't saints or scholars or missionaries. They are tennis players. And they are about to play some astonishing tennis.

CHAPTER ONE

The Outlier

'Arthur and I got to know each other. One time we were both in a junior tournament in Bethesda, Maryland. My father came out near the end of the event and Arthur asked if maybe we could give him a ride back to Washington, DC, and drop him off at the bus station so he could get the bus back to Lynchburg.

'My dad said, "Sure."

'It was a long drive, and all the way Dad kept stopping at Dairy Queen ice-cream stands. It was like a dream come true for a couple of kids, but kind of odd, because Dad was pretty good about what we ate and usually we stopped at restaurants to get decent meals. After we dropped Arthur, I asked Dad why we had stopped so often at Dairy Queens. He said, "I was afraid that if we went into a restaurant with Arthur in tow there might be an incident, and I didn't want to embarrass him."

'Of course I hadn't even thought of that. We weren't really very race-conscious, one way or another. It was just so . . . unusual . . . to even see a black person in those days. We existed in a parallel universe back then in the early 1960s. It was just exotic. Unusual.'

Dick Dell, younger brother of Donald Dell, who was friendly with Ashe when the two were junior players

The boy is just six years old and he is standing well back from the asphalt tennis court at Brook Field, in Richmond, Virginia. He is there almost every day, watching the tennis player named Ronald Charity. The boy, whose name is Arthur Robert Ashe Jr, sees the coach through waves of heat rising from the court. They make the man shimmer and sway on this typical midsummer day when the heat is intense and the humidity stifling.

Ashe is slight, his skin tawny. His legs look like a pair of reeds because he's so thin that some have already taken to calling him 'Skinny', or the slightly more creative 'Bones'. But there is something Ashe likes about the fluidity of this game, tennis. Or perhaps it is just the graceful way this man Charity moves and swings that tennis racquet. The ball comes off it with a pleasant pop.

Charity glides from one side of the court to the other and takes another swing, this time with a high-to-low motion starting above his left shoulder. The racquet face carves at the bottom of the ball, making it spin backwards and sit down nice and low when it alights on the other side of the net. Charity slides back toward the other side, and this time when the ball arrives he takes a big swing and meets it with the racquet face perpendicular to the ground. The ball flies like it was shot from a gun, and Charity's opponent cannot reach it.

There's something Ashe likes about the idea of hitting that fuzzy white ball, over and over. The tennis swing is like a punch; it looks like it feels awful satisfying to connect. And unlike in, say, baseball, you can do it over and over and over. In fact, that appears to be the point. To do it over and over, to punch and hit over and over until one of you misses. Yes, the boy tells himself, he wants to try that. He wants to play that game, and when he gets up the courage he will ask that man to teach him.

Just why and how all this would take such a deep hold on the boy is a mystery as dense and fecund as the atmosphere on this hot summer day in Richmond. For, truth be told, the odds on seeing a black boy in a public park holding a tennis racquet at this point in time are about the same as if he were clutching on to a halibut. Yet there was Young Arthur Ashe Jr, ready to start on what would be a lifelong journey in tennis.

The Ashes of (among other places) Richmond, Virginia, traced their roots back to the mid-eighteenth century, when an 80-ton square rigger christened the *Doddington* brought their descendants over to the New World as slaves. They are a proud family, for over time they acquired a proper family crest painted in bold colors – crimson, black and gold. A broken chain, symbolizing the shattered bonds of slavery, features in the crest, as do clusters of tobacco leaves. The Ashes are, after all, a Southern family.

The last slave in the Ashe lineage was Hammet Blackwell, who married one Julie Tucker. It was a blessed marriage, for it produced twenty-three children – one of whom, Sadie, married a fella named Willie Johnson. Their daughter, Amelia, married Pinkney Avery Ashe, who traced his own progenitors back to slaves owned by Samuel Ashe, an early governor of North Carolina and the man for whom Asheville, NC, was named. Pinkney and Amelia had a son, Arthur, who in 1938 married Mattie 'Baby' Cunningham of Richmond. Their first son, Arthur Jr, was born in 1943. They had another son, Johnnie, five years later.

How do we know all this (and this is just the short version)? Thelma Doswell, a cousin of Arthur Ashe Jr and a teacher of children with learning disabilities, took it upon herself to spend all her spare time for years researching a family tree. When she was finished, she had the entire tree painted onto a six-by-seven-foot canvas containing some 1,500 leaves. One of those leaves – one among the 1,500, and the one representing Arthur Ashe Jr – is painted gold.

Arthur Ashe grew up in South Hill, Va. He had no education past the age of eleven, at which time he lit out for Richmond to make his way in life. He was energetic, gregarious and ambitious. By the age of thirteen he had secured gainful employment as the chauffeur/butler at the home of Mr and Mrs Charles Gregory, earning a salary of $2.50 a week. He dutifully sent all but fifty cents back to his mother in South Hill (the money undoubtedly would come in handy; she would ultimately count 109 children and grandchildren while still in her eighties). Eventually, Arthur went to work for the city of Richmond. He met Mattie 'Baby' Cunningham, who would become his wife, at the Westwood Baptist church.

Mattie Ashe was much like her oldest son, Arthur Jr: quiet, undemonstrative and bookish. She taught him to read when he was four. She died at twenty-seven, leaving her oldest son with but one enduring memory of her alive. It was a powerful remembrance that remained with Ashe all his life. He could still see Mattie standing at the door of their home at Brook Field in a blue corduroy bathrobe, waving goodbye to Arthur Jr as he left one day to go ramble in the park.

Ordinarily, she would have been at work at Miller and Rhoads' department store, but she had only recently given birth to Johnnie, and she was scheduled to have minor surgery for an infection related to her pregnancy. Later that day. Arthur took her to the hospital from which she would never return. In later years, Arthur would talk about how a blue jay in an oak tree near the house began to sing that day, and wouldn't relent despite Arthur firing rocks at the bird and, in desperation, a warning shot from his .38 caliber revolver. Five days later, when Mattie died, the bird fell silent.

Later in life, relatives would tell Arthur Jr that he had 'withdrawn' after her death. One of his aunts, he would write, even said: 'Arthur was so small and pathetic. He looked like a motherless child. It about near broke my heart.' But at the time Mattie died, Arthur told his son many years later that, while he sat crying his eyes out with infant Johnnie on one side and Arthur Jr on the other, Arthur Jr turned to him, dry-eyed, and said, 'Don't cry, Daddy.'

Arthur Jr is a sickly boy who has periodic bouts with childhood illnesses including mumps, measles and whooping cough. That he has no mother for much of his youth is somewhat alleviated by the fact that his father is a deeply involved parent. But he is, after all, a man – a certain kind of man, too. He drives a truck, swings a hammer, collects parts from defunct auto-mobiles and enjoys fishing and hunting. He's not the type of fellow who's likely to dote on a skinned knee, or take alarm when his son has the sniffles or forgets to wear a sweatshirt on a chilly day. He is also a man many kids would love to have as a father because one of the perks of his job as the superintendent of Brook Field, a blacks-only public park with a swimming pool and all manner of athletic fields, is that his family gets to live in the caretaker's cottage, which is smack dab in the middle of the park. For the frail but athletic Arthur Jr, this is rather like being a drinking man who lives in a pub.

But Arthur is a tough disciplinarian who takes extra care to ensure that, history and simmering notions of 'social justice' be damned, his sons don't develop a smoldering resentment toward white folks. This is a profoundly practical decision by a man who's built a life upon them. He's seen many 'Negro' men (the adjective 'black' had not yet become popular) ruin their lives because they carried that enormously heavy chip of the past on their shoulders, and he's not about to let his boys succumb to the idea that the world owes them a living – or even, for that matter, an apology. He doesn't mind that some Negroes, those 'uppity' kind, consider him a hustler, an Oreo (like the cookie, black on the outside but white on the inside), or even an 'Uncle Tom'. He knows what he knows, and one thing he knows is that you don't get anywhere in this world if you hold grudges or don't respect others – even those who show you little or no respect themselves.

The Ashes are not poor, and Arthur Jr and Johnnie are spared the kind of bone-chilling experiences and hardships that other African Americans experience. Young Johnnie and Arthur might not have felt that way, given how their father makes them go down for a midday nap every day, and prevails upon them to eat sandwiches only on unappealing if healthy wholewheat bread and to brush their teeth with baking soda. But such is the scope of a child's concerns.

While Virginia remains a stronghold of segregation, the blacks who live there are spared some of the squalor and soul-killing features of life that exist in the cold, northern ghettos. Whites in the north talk a good game when it comes to integration and racial equality, but the facts on the ground point toward their hypocrisy and a more subtly refined brand of racism as much as they do toward color-blindness or enlightened integration. The north does breed a more outspoken, aware black man, and Arthur Jr is destined to deal with him. But in the south in the 1950s fear of white power and the tradition of southern manners, which influences all races and classes, tends to suppress the expression of overt antagonisms – even if that doesn't automatically equate with feelings of genuine brotherhood.

In any event, Arthur is not merely a philosopher when it comes to his children. On Arthur Jr's first day of school his father walks him to the door of the George F. Baker Elementary School at his son's pace, carefully noting how minutes the trip takes. Later, he tells Arthur Jr that he best make it home in the same amount of time. When Arthur Jr wants to earns some pocket money (and, presumably, broaden his horizons beyond the confines of Brook Field) and asks if he can sign up for a route delivering newspapers, Arthur says no. Later, when Arthur Jr goes to visit a young lady he knows from the Westwood Baptist Church and fails to show up at home promptly upon his 11 p.m. curfew, Arthur goes to fetch him. Thanks partly to his convictions and the inflexible way he cleaves to them, Arthur will eventually become a Special Police Officer in the Department of

Recreation and Parks, a promotion that will entitle him to carry a nightstick, handcuffs and a handgun.

On weekends, Arthur and his sons drive around Richmond, scavenging building materials from which they will eventually build a house (one of the five Arthur will come to own and eventually make his family's home) in Gum Spring, a town about thirty-five miles north-west of Richmond. Arthur Jr doesn't enjoy these forays, nor all the time he spends helping his dad mix cement, install wiring and pull nails. He has no aspirations to be, like his father, a jack of all trades. Instead, Arthur Jr will become a master of one.

He has been watching the man Ronald Charity with the attention of a hawk for days upon days and hours on end. Now Arthur Ashe Jr finally gets up the nerve to ask the man who handles that tennis racquet so expertly and moves so gracefully if he might consider teaching him to play. Charity is one of perhaps two dozen black men in Richmond who play tennis. As a college freshman, he became interested in tennis and bought a book, Lloyd Budge's *Tennis Made Easy*. He moved on to books by Alice Marble and, finally, William 'Big Bill' Tilden, considered at that time the greatest of all players.

But tennis is a game in which a player is heavily depend-ent on the existence of other players of roughly the same level of skill. Charity knows that Richmond is short of tennis players. He sees the young Ashe boy as a recruit. He wonders about the boy's strength and stamina, an understandable worry, given that for obvious reasons the youngster's nicknames are 'Skinny', 'Bones' and 'Ears'. But he gives the child a racquet and shows him how to assume the continental grip, the one favored by icons such as Australia's Rod Laver and Tony Roche. It isn't the most natural feeling grip, but Ashe obediently adopts it. At first, Charity stands just six feet from the thin boy and gently tosses him balls. But Ashe is a surprisingly quick learner. In no time at all, Charity retreats to the far side of the net, upping the ante. Now the balls Ashe hits must travel over the net. Soon he will have to keep them inside the lines as well. And as the days blend into weeks and then into months, Charity actually finds himself doing drills with Ashe – requiring the youngster to hit five or ten or twenty-five forehands cross-court, followed by the same number of backhands down the line. He saves the drills for the evening, when it is nice and cool.

In this endeavor, Charity is instilling muscle memory in his protégé. He is also trying to impress on Ashe a cardinal rule that Ashe will be accused of breaking, with gusto, for his entire life: Charity wants Ashe to understand how important it is to be consistent. To be able to hit the same shot, over and over, instead of blazing away in a frequently vain attempt to end a point by making a winner. He wants Ashe to practice each shot until it is second nature. To color inside the lines.

The boy seems surprisingly amenable to all of this, even though by nature he will always be a bold and at times almost reckless shot-maker. The gratification in doing these drills and long, exhausting practice sessions is that Ashe gets to hit that ball, gets to feel the satisfying give in the felt-covered rubber ball and in the strings of his racquet, over and over and over again. It releases something in him. It makes him feel good. It doesn't hurt anyone.

When Charity, who also teaches tennis in the afternoons at the park, is otherwise occupied or elsewhere, Ashe plays against the one opponent nobody has ever beaten, the practice backboard. If anyone is looking for a hit or a game, Ashe is happy to oblige. It's easy to get frustrated when you play hour after hour. You can become overloaded, like a child who's had too much sugar and has stayed up late. Once, while practicing at Brook Field, Ashe is so disgusted by an error he makes that he flings his racquet at the ground in frustration. Seemingly before it even clatters on the asphalt, he hears a screen door slam and here comes his father. It is the last time anyone sees Arthur Ashe Jr hurl a racquet.

Ronald Charity and a group of like-minded tennis enthusiasts belong to the Richmond Racquet Club. Although they all are grown men, they welcome Arthur Ashe Jr into their company. This expands Ashe's base of hitting partners and gives him more places to play. But perhaps most of all it gives him a sense of belonging. Despite his aloof, watchful manner and natural reticence, he would be a social creature all his life, some-one comfortable belonging to and working with a group of like-minded individuals. He is comfortable in the company of the men who make up the Richmond Racquet Club. His game grows by leaps and bounds, and he begins to attract attention.

One day, Ashe is hitting with a regular partner. Ashe makes a cracking good shot – perhaps it is one of the rifle-shot backhands for which he will one day become famous – and Charity observes that Ashe is taking a quick look to see who else might have seen the winner. Whereupon Charity sits the young man down and delivers a lecture on showboating. It culminates in a warning: I catch you doing that again and I'm not going to bother with you any more. Ashe's career as a swaggerer is over. He's not quite ten years old, but he's a quick learner who enjoys school as well as tennis. Charity realizes that he's stumbled across someone really special, and he decides to get in touch with a Lynchburg physician by the name of Robert Walter Johnson, MD.

By 1953, Ronald Charity was recently graduated from Virginia Union University and a ranking player in the American Tennis Association, or ATA, an organization of African American tennis players created in 1916 as their own equivalent to the ruling body of organized American tennis, the United States Lawn Tennis Association (the

'Lawn' has since been dropped from the name). He has also been the mentor of Arthur Ashe Jr for about four years, and he knows that Ashe has a unique set of skills ideal for excelling at tennis. Ashe is a pretty good baseball pitcher, but he's not big enough for football, nor fast enough to excel at track. But his eye-hand coordination is marvelous, his reflexes excellent and his temperament highly suitable to a game as mentally intense as tennis. Still, all that would not be enough. Ashe also has a phenomenal capacity for work, for improving.

There is only so much Charity can do for Ashe; there are no agents or clothing and shoe companies willing to write big checks that might enable Charity to make a living as Ashe's coach and mentor. There is, however, an African American doctor who has been running a kind of tennis academy for a number of years now, and Charity decides to give him a call.

Like the Ashes, Dr Robert Walter Johnson was the descendant of slaves. In his case, though, one of his forebears was an indentured white slave named Nancy Scott. Her granddaughter, also named Nancy, had light skin and long, black hair. She married Jerry Johnson, a hard-working black man she first met at a carnival outside Plymouth, North Carolina, in 1895. They had six children, including Robert, and were the first black family in Plymouth to enjoy indoor plumbing, electricity and, ultimately, an automobile.

Young Robert, blessed with the same degree of drive

and energy that powered his father Jerry's prosperity, was an exceptional athlete. By the time he was of college age, Johnson was known far and wide in African American circles as 'Whirlwind', a nickname bestowed upon him by admirers of his exploits on the football field. He was the highest scoring player in records of the Colored Intercollegiate Athletic Association, and once scored forty-eight points in a single game.

Whirlwind might also be a useful adjective to describe the progress Robert Walter Johnson made through the ranks of Virginia's finest and most desirable ladies. By the age of seventeen he stood accused of fathering the child of a young girl. Although Robert claimed that she enjoyed congress with other men as well, Jerry and Nancy agreed to help support the child. This was just the beginning of Whirlwind's long and colorful career as a Lothario, an abiding interest for most of his life – and one that would cause considerable distress to his family.

Johnson also loved poker: he was kicked out of Virginia Union University for playing the game, a friend once claimed to see him bet $400 on a pair of tens, and he once lost a car during a particularly brutal losing streak. Later, in 1932, Johnson earned his degree from Meharry Medical College in Nashville, Tennessee. He was thirty-five years old when he started his own practice in Lynchburg, Va. He feared at the time that because he had built up large heart muscles through vigorous athletics he would have to remain active in order to avoid fatty infiltration. He discovered tennis and in no time he realized it was a game at which he could become good but never fully master. In other words, he was hooked.

One reason tennis appealed to Johnson was obvious. As Doug Smith points out in his important book, *Whirlwind: The Godfather of Black Tennis*, Johnson was an upper-crust African-American whose father had been a highly successful entrepreneur. At the time, successful blacks often tried to define their superiority by the degree to which they resembled whites (or perhaps it was merely how different they looked from dark-skinned 'pure blood' Negroes), or how conversantly they affected the habits and interests of those whites living out there in the parallel universe. The light-skinned or straighter-haired progeny of plantation owners and their sons received special benefits. They often served as house staff, absolved from the brutal work in the fields. And they considered themselves superior to those laborers.

Consequently, any union of couples with different shades of skin was considered either marrying up – or down (Arthur Ashe Jr would confess that there were examples of this prejudice even in his own family). Whirlwind Johnson, a charismatic fellow and superb athlete, was unlikely to be hamstrung by such unspoken dictums. Annie Pate, the sixteen-year-old North Carolina girl who would become Whirlwinds's wife, was described as having 'good skin and nice color' – code for light-skinned and all that implied in terms of genealogy. For this, she was a great catch, much as Whirlwind's mother Nancy, the daughter of a house servant, had been for her dark-skinned suitor Jerry, whose own daddy had worked in the fields. Predictably, the higher you climbed on the African American social ladder, the more significant such distinctions became. And Whirlwind, Dr Walter Johnson, was breathing very thin air by the time he decided to build a tennis court in his backyard in the late 1930s.

As his practice grew, Johnson's reputation as a mover and shaker in tennis did as well. Among African Americans his reputation as a doctor vied with his fame for having a basement that was the equal of any nightclub, complete with red leather banquettes and blue-tinted mirrors. The room became the epicenter of his annual Labor Day ATA tennis tournament – an invitational affair spiced up on at least one occasion by the presence of gorgeous young women imported from Cuba.

All this sits in apposition to how conservative and discipline-oriented Johnson was in the role destined to earn him a share of tennis immortality. For by 1951, he was so committed to the dream of producing an African American boy who could win the USLTA inter-scholastic championships that he had started what may be the very first example of what has come to be known as a 'tennis academy'.

*

In 1953, Charity takes young Arthur to visit Dr Johnson for a tryout. When they arrive, they are treated to a tour of Johnson's property. His house is spacious, two-stories tall with four upstairs bedrooms. Behind Johnson's house is a garage and tool shed, chock-a-block with just about every teaching aid and contraption created in the endless pursuit of making it easier to hit an effective forehand, or a cannonball serve. Johnson calls his cadre of eight or ten promising young players the Junior Development Team.

In its own way, this setup is at least as impressive as Whirlwind's basement lounge, albeit in an utterly different way and with utterly different purpose. It's a tribute to the DIY sensibility. If Johnson were a Second World War aviation buff, he might have been tempted to build a B-52 bomber out of spare parts in his basement. The garage is equipped with 'The Tom Stow Stroke Developer' invented by the teacher of J. Donald Budge, the first man to record a Grand Slam (a sweep of all four major tournaments: the Australian, French and US National Championships plus Wimbledon, the de facto British championships). It's a surprisingly primitive device: an elastic cord to which a sliding tennis ball is attached. Johnson's students hone their eye-hand coordination by whacking at the ball with a sawn-off section of broomstick.

The first impression the whippet-lean ten-year-old makes on Dr Johnson is not very favorable. The doctor considers him an unfortunate specimen, and his medical training leads him to speculate that the boy may have suffered from rickets. Johnson worries that when Ashe runs and hits a shot the effort will knock him down. Yet . . . something about Ashe's persistence, his discipline and his apparent willingness to learn strikes a chord in Johnson, who agrees to take him on as a live-in protégé. Ashe becomes the junior member in a group from which Johnson hopes to cull a youngster capable of winning the national high school championships.

The course of his future set, Ashe returns home and soon he is at the Greyhound bus station in Richmond, clutching a bag containing his personal articles and racquet, ready to board the bus to Lynchburg. When he gets on, he sees that the best seat – the one across the aisle from the driver – is vacant. A curious child tingling inside with a feeling that he's going on a great adventure, he's eager to see the countryside. He takes the vacant seat only to have the driver look over at him and, in a kind voice, say: 'Now, son, you know you can't sit there.' Ashe takes his stuff and moves to the back of the bus.

Up until this point in his young life, Ashe has been vaguely aware of segregation, but he has not had much first-hand experience with it. To this point, the boundaries of his young life have been those of Brook Field, a place where, when he wasn't banging a ball against the wall, he was cavorting with friends in the pool, or roughhousing on the football field, his father an omnipresent and unquestionable figure of authority who gave Arthur Jr an extra measure of status at the park. Now, he was butting up against a different world. Just how different he would soon find out.

'We are going into a different world,' Johnson is fond of telling his pupils, referring to his intention to crack the color barrier in tennis. In junior tennis, the players in the early rounds are usually responsible for calling their own lines. Therefore, he insists that if a ball hit by an opponent is anywhere near the line (or seemingly two inches behind it), his player must accept it as good. Johnson knows that whites consider blacks emotional and childlike, so he insists that there be no tantrums, racquet hurling, or outbursts. He sees his protégés as a kind of lab experiment. He has faith that they can master the sport and storm the bastion of white superiority.

Most of this is fine with Ashe. He hasn't thrown a racquet since that day back in Brook Field. He's never been one to start hollering and carrying on when he's frustrated. This business of playing on or giving up a point when he knows darned well he's won? It doesn't sit well with him, but so be it. The thing that sticks in his craw is having to clean out the kennel where Dr Johnson keeps his hunting dogs. Dr Johnson pretends it is no big deal; all anyone has to do is hose down the concrete floor. As a junior member of the Development

Team, Arthur has no real choice, while his fellow students get to do more appealing and less fragrant chores, like weeding the garden and spraying the apple trees with pesticides.

Ashe has one crisis while he is under the tutelage of Dr Johnson, and it almost costs him his 'scholarship'. Just a few days into his stay, Ashe is working out with the man who does most of the teaching, Johnson's son Robert. Instructed to do something a certain way, Ashe balks and finally tells Robert that what he wants is contrary to what Ronald Charity believes. His pride stung, Robert reports to his father, who also takes exception to Ashe's attitude and decides that he is more trouble than he is worth. He calls Arthur Ashe and suggests that he come down and get his son.

Arriving in Lynchburg, Arthur marches on to the court and asks his son, point-blank, if he wants to stay with Dr Johnson. When Arthur Jr avows that he does, his father orders him to do everything Dr Johnson or Robert say, regardless. The lesson is not lost on Arthur Jr. He becomes putty in the Johnsons' hands, executing every directive at any price. Overnight, and thanks perhaps to the authority of his father and the black and white way he exercises it, Arthur becomes a model student.

Johnson's ascetic view of proper conduct and healthy living are not all reflexive responses to the challenge he's undertaken. He believes deeply in the kind of discipline he could not be accused of having cultivated in his own robust youth. Junk food is forbidden the boys, and their diet is loaded up with vegetables and, at most meals, a choice of meats. The boys make their beds, hang up their clothes and stand up when a lady enters the room (infrequent an occurrence as that was). They receive instruction in manners as well as tennis. Johnson wants his students fully prepared to meet whatever test the 'new world' he so often refers to has in store, even when it blindsides them at a set dinner table by presenting them with two or three different kinds of forks, each intended for a different use.

Ashe adapts to Dr Johnson's regimen better than most, and he is awed by the man and his apparent wealth. And while he loves the daily training sessions and intense, intra-team competition, he hates just about everything else about the life he's been thrust into. The winning, though, is intoxicating. In the beginning, he is the least competent kid on the team. But the Johnsons notice that he is always the last to leave the court, and that he has a great capacity for improvement. By the time Ashe is fifteen, his promise as a player is abundant – and obvious. This only makes Johnson push harder; some days he demands that Ashe hit 500 serves before he is allowed breakfast. Johnson's criticism is sometimes harsh. Ashe often becomes discouraged, and toys with the idea of quitting. But Johnson lectures him and asks if he has the character and capacity to 'endure'. One of Ashe's stablemates, Horace Cunningham, routinely beats Ashe in practice. Yet when the boys begin to travel to tournaments and the two meet, it is Ashe who wins. This ability to perform under pressure is something that cannot really be taught, and Ashe appears to have it.

As Ashe becomes a player to be reckoned with, Johnson decides to enter him in some of the more significant junior events, the ones that matter when it comes to earning a sectional or even a national ranking (the USLTA itself is composed of seventeen sections along regional lines). The results are mixed. Officials of Ashe's own section, Middle Atlantic Lawn Tennis Association (MALTA), refuse to process his application to play in an important event to be held at the Country Club of Virginia — right in Ashe's home town of Richmond. Thus Ashe was unable to get a ranking in the MALTA section even when he was already ranked no. 5 in the nation. In 1959, when Ashe is sixteen and destined to play in his first national championships (what would become the US Open), he tries to enter the MALTA championships that will be held at the Congressional Country Club in Bethesda, Md. He is informed that his application arrived 'too late'.

Ashe makes some inroads, though. He makes friends, many of them kids like Dick Dell, who are less conscious of race, or conscious of it in a different way than their parents. They just see Ashe's talent and they are awed by it. What else could possibly matter to a youngster? And yes, he even looks different; he's a Negro. Not very black, but a black man. They may not know what to make of him, but they aren't even prepared or equipped to try. They don't really have to, because he's one hell of a tennis player. That much they can see, and what else matters?

The ball rolls on to the court at the worst possible moment for Arthur Ashe Jr. He is up a set and 4-3 on top-seeded Billy Lenoir in the quarter-finals of the 1960 USLTA Interscholastic Championships in Charlottesville, Va. It is the same place and event that Dr Walter Johnson happened to stumble upon while driving by on that June day of 1949. The same sight that inspired Johnson to try developing, come hell or high water, a black boy who could compete on an equal footing and perhaps even triumph over all those admittedly talented, smooth white youngsters.

Eleven years later, the most gifted player to come out of Johnson's Junior Development Team is seeded no. 8 in the official national high school championships, and he's on the verge of beating the most dangerous player in the draw. And the damned ball rolls on to the court just as Arthur wins the point that would give him a 5-3 lead – one game from pulling off an upset.

Ashe has changed much since he showed up on Johnson's doorstep, so frail that a puff of wind threatened to knock him over. One thing that hasn't changed, though, is Ashe's unspoken covenant with Johnson, a pledge sealed on the day Arthur's father showed up at Johnson's and informed his son that if he wanted to stay in Lynchburg, he would have to yield unequivocally to Dr Johnson's designs. One of those designs was the doctor's insistence that his charges play by the rules, and give opponents the benefit of the doubt in any disagreement. This mandate had much to do with the delicate issue of race, but wittingly or not it also had much to do with sportsmanship – a concept that tennis people, for all their sins and irrespective of race, creed or color – valued.

Up close to the net at the end of the point, Ashe sees the ball roll in from another court behind Lenoir. He does the right thing: 'Did that ball bother you?'

According to Dr Johnson's later, written account, Lenoir gives an answer of which any lawyer might be proud. He says, 'The referee said to always play a point over if a ball comes on the court from another court.'

Ashe doesn't like it, but Lenoir has him dead to rights. He agrees to play the point over. Naturally, Ashe loses it. The incident plays on his mind, and he allows his advantage to slip away. It's the kind of thing that happens in tennis all the time. Ashe is unable to shake the sense that something terrible has happened to him. That he knows he ought to be ahead by 5-3 only makes it worse. Lenoir wins the second set. In the pit of his stomach, Ashe knows he will lose this match. He does his best to clear his head, to hit the reset button. He knows that's what he needs to do, he knows that's what he cannot do. Lenoir wins the third set.

This is a setback, but on the whole it has been a momentous, thrilling year. Dr Johnson, though, continues to feel lingering prejudice in Virginia, but he is also aware that Ashe has outgrown Lynchburg and the Junior Development Team. In fact, there is nobody in the whole state, black or white, who can provide the level of competition Ashe needs. So Dr Johnson places his loyal, star pupil with the family of a St Louis-based friend and ally in the ATA leadership, Richard Hudlin.

Ashe does not want to go to St Louis. He is loath to leave Richmond's Maggie Walker High School where, among other things, he pals around with the geeks and nerds and harbors a monstrous crush on an algebra teacher named Miss Austin.

Like Johnson, Hudlin has a tennis court in his backyard. But the great benefit of living in St Louis is that Ashe, fresh from his triumph in both the junior and men's ATA championships of 1960, gets to practice with some of the nation's top juniors, including Chuck McKinley and Butch and Cliff Buchholz. Moreover, while there was little indoor tennis to be had in Virginia in the winter, Ashe and his young rivals get to play on the wooden floor of the St Louis Armory. This enables Ashe to develop the serve and volley game that would stand him – and many others of his generation – in good stead. In November, while attending Sumner High

School, Ashe wins his first national title, the junior indoor championships.

After Ashe graduates from all-black Sumner High School in St Louis with the best grades in his class, he returns to Lynchburg with his retooled, more aggressive game. Dr Johnson fires up the plush Buick and drives Arthur up to Charlottesville, the scene of his painful meltdown twelve months earlier against Billy Lenoir. This time, Ashe slashes his way through the draw without losing a set to win the USLTA National Interscholastics. After twelve long years, Dr Johnson's mission is complete, and for the first time in his life he allows himself to think that maybe, just maybe, a black man can one day win the US National Championships up in New York.

Late in the interscholastic tournament, several of Ashe's white friends, including Cliff Buchholz (whom Ashe defeated in the semi-finals), Charlie Pasarell and Butch Newman, invite Ashe to join them to see a movie. They are turned away at the ticket booth, an exasperated Ashe uncharacteristically asking what he must do to enable the party to enter: paint himself with whitewash? Ashe's white friends decide that if he can't go in, they won't go in. They decide to go shoot pool instead. The decision makes Ashe happy; he feels he has genuine friends among the whites, and he remembers his father's cautionary words about that destructive emotion, bitterness.

Ashe will go on to play the summer circuit in the US before he embarks on his college education at UCLA.

Lynchburg is behind him now, and in some ways he feels like a truly free man. Two details pertaining to his future in tennis stand out, although neither Ashe nor the two men in germane to the situation can know it.

The first black Johnson protégé to distinguish himself in the USLTA Interscholastic Championships at Charlottesville was a boy named Willie Winn. In 1952, he surprised everyone by winning two rounds. The man who finally stopped him was Donald Dell.

The man who informed Dr Johnson by mail that Ashe's entry into the MALTA championships of 1959 had been rejected on the grounds of lateness was Bill Riordan.

CHAPTER TWO

The Outsider

'I've been known as a pushy stage-door mother, but my biggest problem was to stop him from playing tennis. He's always been the same. Why, he couldn't wait to kick the slats out of his playpen and get started in life. But always a homebody. Johnny would like to spend the night at other boys' houses. Not Jimmy. He was so happy just being in his own home. You know, he was so much like his grandmother especially. We were a team. We were three peas in a pod.'

Gloria Connors, to *Sports Illustrated* writer
Frank Deford

It's a quiet Sunday in 2010 and the old reluctance is still upon the man as he parks his car and walks toward the church and up the steps, his hip replacements forcing him to move more gingerly than his past as a champion would suggest. But he no longer even remembers his original hips; three surgeries on one or the other joint have left him toting around a fair amount of titanium where there once was real bone and cartilage.

The man has a jowly face. His eyes recede into mere black slits when he smiles. His hair is now swept up and back, rakishly parted in the middle. He trained it that way through many perming sessions in a hair salon. He was born Irish Catholic, but he has never had much use for all the rigmarole of the faith; he's always been a rebel and in his heart he probably still sees himself as such. He does not attend church on Sundays to commune with God, or to take stock of his own failings, or those of the world. He is there to talk to his mother, Gloria Connors. She is not at the organist's bench or in the front pew; she is in the next, presumably better, world.

When he sits he will ask her how she kept him interested in tennis in the early years, when the kids his age were bigger and better. How did she know he really would 'grow into' his game? Did he get his own defiant attitude from her 'fuck it' attitude toward anything that interfered with his game? These are things he still thinks and talks about in those silent conversations with Gloria. For him, there really is no, as they like to say nowadays, 'moving on'. There never will be, not from this. Not from what he and his mother accomplished together through the strength of her will and, of course, the terrible power of her love.

*

James Scott Connors was born in East St Louis, Mo., almost exactly nine years after Arthur Ashe Jr, not very far from where Ashe lived when he was sent to stay with the Hudlins and finish his senior year of high school. Ashe honed his volleying and serving skills on the polished hardwood floor of a St Louis national guard armory during the winter months; almost a decade later, Connors would sharpen up his counter-punching skills — and his older brother John would steal an army jeep — during the cold months in the same building.

Gloria and Jimmy Connors would enjoy a close relationship. Yet the son's most outstanding memory of his mother, like Ashe's sole remembrance of his own, is more than doleful — it's horrifying. And it left so strong an impression that many years later he would begin his autobiography by reliving it. He would describe in detail the way his mother was savagely beaten by local thugs who fell upon her while she was giving a lesson to John and eight-year-old Jimmy on a public court in Jones Park, East St Louis.

Almost all of Gloria's teeth are knocked out in that assault, and her father, Jimmy's beloved grandfather, Al Lynch 'Pop' Thompson, who is the chief of the local parks police and a former Golden Gloves middleweight boxer, is also badly beaten. The reconstruction of Gloria's mouth requires hundreds of stitches, and it will cause her to live with a measure of pain and discomfort for the rest of her life. Later that evening, Gloria's husband 'Big Jim' Connors returns to Jones Park with Johnny and Jimmy to comb the court in search of her teeth. They figure, what the heck, they might be able to put them back or something.

The next morning, Gloria is resting on the couch. Johnny and Jimmy, oblivious as only children can be, ask if she wants to go and hit some tennis balls. She gets up, takes the boys into the backyard and they hit some balls. The awful incident, however, leaves a lasting impression on the boys. Jimmy will often trace the anger and rage that suddenly wells up inside him throughout his life back to that day in Jones Park. Gloria understands those feelings in her favorite son, and she finds a good use for them. She even gives them a name, so that Jimmy – or 'Jimbo' as she is beginning to call him – will not forget. She calls them 'tiger juices', and neither Gloria nor Jimbo appear troubled by how the name may, to some, evoke thoughts of some strange bodily fluid, may even sound gross, or even vaguely sexual. Gloria and Jimbo don't give a damn what the world thinks, for they see themselves as 'outsiders' living a perpetual struggle in an 'us vs them' world.

Pop Thompson is part of the small 'us' group, but Big Jim Connors is not. Bertha Thompson, Pop's wife, Gloria's mother and Jimmy's co-coach (he calls her 'Two-Mom') is an 'us', while all the other tennis players on Planet Earth, young and old, are 'thems'. Jimmy's brother Johnny is an 'us' – at least for the time being, but later, when he steals a lot of money from Jimmy, he will become something of a 'them'.

The feeling that they are preyed upon and besieged, that the world is poised against them, helps stiffen the resistance and resolve of the outsiders. The sense that they are either of a lower class, or seen as such by the 'them', fuels their resentments. The conviction that they must fight for everything they extract from life only makes the outsiders more determined to get their share (there simply are no bluebird days, beautiful and freely given by nature; none of those famous 'acts of senseless beauty and random kindness' practiced upon them). The grotesque irony is that they are outsiders mainly in their view, not the eyes of the world. But perhaps it is always that way. And perhaps it serves Gloria's purposes and ambitions.

Tennis and golf, sports pursued by individuals, are radically different from our popular team sports. They tend to be family- rather than playground- or school-based. Serious tennis players travel in the same circles. They become acquainted and compete against each other from a young age onward, sometimes for fifteen or twenty years, sometimes even for multiple generations. Football or basketball players on a school team rarely know anyone on the team they play once a year on a given Saturday, and usually pass out of each other's lives as swiftly as they entered.

For those and other reasons, tennis and other sports like it create large, generation-spanning subcultures. It's common to see the offspring of former high-level players in the draw at a tournament, or even out on the field courts, competing in the junior championship of Wimbledon or the US Open. This subculture is also surprisingly diverse, and it gives a lie to the trope that tennis is a sport of the rich (it hardly matters, for that conviction has proven indestructible and impervious to evidence). Tennis, especially at the higher levels of the game, is by and large a sport of tennis nuts who span the entire socio-economic spectrum. But it's also undeniable that newcomers to the game are usually attracted to the tennis esthetic, which has also been associated with bourgeois gentility and prosperity.

If you can see past the all-white clothing rule and mannerly rituals that smack of the gentry, tennis is also the ultimate democratic game, and one in which an army of one can conquer the world. Once the players step on to the court there is no advantage whatsoever for the rich kid over the poor one. The only real outsiders in tennis are those who self-identify as such. The mystifying thing is why Gloria Connors is so intent on impressing upon Jimmy his outsider status when she could just as easily celebrate her family's involvement in the tennis community.

Bertha 'Two Mom' Thompson, Gloria's mother, was smitten by tennis after taking her first two swipes at the ball on a court in East St Louis. Self-taught, much like Arthur Ashe's original mentors, she became a known figure in the neighborhood tennis circles. She taught Pop Thompson to play and together they won several local mixed doubles tournaments. By the early 1940s, Two-Mom was a highly ranked player in the Missouri Valley section of the USLTA.

Two-Mom passed her game on to daughter Gloria, who played the Missouri Valley sectional circuit as a teenager and won a number of titles, including some in doubles alongside her mother. In 1939, the inevitable came to pass, and the two women met in singles in the semi-finals of a significant invitational tournament in Kansas City. At the time, Gloria Thompson was just fifteen. But Bertha happened to be short of the milk of human kindness that day and clobbered her daughter, 6-0, 6-0.

That proved to be no more traumatic for Gloria than such beatings inflicted by the hand of his mother would be for Jimmy. Gloria would go on to become the youngest player, at sixteen, to compete in the prestigious Western Open tournament in Indianapolis. Over the next few years, she would play in the US National Championships (which would become the US Open in 1968) twice. Gloria then moved to Los Angeles, where she lived with her best friend – and a superior player

who would go on to win five Grand Slam singles titles
– Pauline Betz. The women played on the professional
circuit, and when Gloria wasn't otherwise engaged she
taught tennis to kids and coached celebrities, including
Mickey Rooney and Errol Flynn.

This represented a great leap up the social ladder of
tennis for the Thompson women. Gloria had penetrated
the highest echelon of the tennis's incestuous subculture.
Among other things, she dated Jimmy Evert, whose
own daughter, Chris, would ultimately be engaged to
Gloria's Jimbo. If anything, Gloria Thompson had established her place among the insiders. But her intricate,
circular web of relationships was shattered when Pop
Thompson called and told his midwestern, Catholic
daughter that it was time to come home to East St Louis.
Time to think of starting a family.

Obediently, Gloria returned to her home town.
Before long, she met Big Jim Connors, who was a far cry
from Errol Flynn but considerably taller and sexier than
Mickey Rooney. Before long, they wed and soon settled
into separate lives.

Johnny and Jimmy are eight and six years old respectively,
and they're having one of their occasional dinners at the
Paddock Lounge, which is owned by Buster Wortman, a
friend of Jimmy's late grandfather, John T. Connors.
Unbeknownst to the children, Wortman is also a

bootlegger, gambler and the member of a Prohibition-era gang, the Shelton Brothers.

While the Connors are eating, a gang of men bursts through the front door and flushes a quartet of men from their seats at a nearby table.

Bang! Bang! Bang! Jimmy never does see what happens, because some of Wortman's 'associates' whisk his family away into the protection of the kitchen. It turns out to be a case of mistaken identity; the shooters were hoping to kill Wortman, although it's doubtful that the four victims took much consolation from that.

John T. Connors was a municipal fixture in East St Louis; he died before Gloria's youngest was born, but years later Jimmy would speculate that he was quite a 'mover and shaker'. John T. had been police commissioner and, later, mayor, at a time when East St Louis was anything but the decaying, post-industrial city it became by the time Jimmy Connors put it on the map.

In John T's time, the Mississippi river, rail lines and local stockyards were all doing brisk business with Chicago. That made for a lot of moving and shaking, but apparently much of the shimmying by John T. occurred on the wrong side of the law. In 1947, John T. Connors was among the nineteen city officials indicted for malfeasance. Apparently they were looking the other way when it came to illegal gambling, and had no particular interest in redressing election irregularities.

John T.'s son, 'Big Jim' Connors, was certainly privileged, and he went to the college where all good Irish Catholic kids most wanted to go, Notre Dame. His education was interrupted by the Second World War, and Big Jim joined the US Air Force, serving, according to Jimmy, as a 'bomber instructor'. Big Jim had no great appetite for completing his education when the war was over; he never did finish college.

Big Jim was a handsome, nicely proportioned, sharply dressed and relatively sophisticated man. He swept Gloria off her feet and, perhaps partly because of his status in those parts, she agreed to marry him in a heartbeat. Jimmy remembers it as an idyllic union until 1951, the year Johnny was born. Gloria, who had enjoyed making the social rounds in East St Louis as much as anyone, embraced her responsibilities as a mother and made a seemingly easy transition to caregiver and stay-at-home mom. Big Jim, however, wasn't about to start spending his evenings crawling around on the carpet or wiping baby vomit off his shirt front. Always a *bon vivant*, he continued to enjoy a carefree nightlife with his many friends.

Although an ectoptic pregnancy with Johnny followed by a string of miscarriages had doctors warning Gloria that she ought never to risk bearing a child again, little Jimmy was born on 2 September 1952. In his mother's own words, he was diminutive and seemed fragile. She would tell him in later years that he looked like a 'little dishrag'.

In the ensuing years, Gloria and Big Jim would grow increasingly estranged. Much would be made in later years over how Big Jim was virtually banished from the Connors family. He never did see his son play a match in person, perhaps because in the early years when Jimmy's ascent was exciting, Gloria traveled everywhere with Jimmy. The press had a field day when they learned that Big Jim had called to congratulate his son when Jimmy first won Wimbledon in 1972, reporting that Jimmy never took or returned the call. Jimmy later claimed that he had spoken with his father that day – at some later point.

Big Jim has been frequently described, often with barely suppressed derision, as the toll collector on Veteran's Bridge, a Mississippi crossing that connected St Louis, Missouri, and East St Louis, which is in Illinois. It's always been part of the 'blue-collar' Connors narrative. But few of the reports mention that Big Jim was the manager of the toll booth, or that he came by the position through an act of nepotism.

John T., upon realizing that his son had no intention of returning to Notre Dame when he was released from the service, installed Big Jim in that position. Something about operating the toll booth, where the essential business was handling large sums of cash in small doses, suited Big Jim. It certainly impressed his children. Jimmy remembers that Johnny at about the age of ten would return from a day helping his father at the toll booth with pockets sagging from their cargo of dimes and quarters. The mayor's son enjoyed his job and its benefits so thoroughly that he kept at it until the day he died in January 1977.

Jimmy claimed in later years that, while his father was something of a family outcast, he was proud of all Jimmy accomplished, and had provided reliable material support for the family when the boys were children. Some of Big Jim's 'contacts' in the building trade went as far as building him a house that enabled the Connors to move from East St Louis to the more desirable town of Belleville in 1964. Big Jim's marriage with Gloria, however, appeared to be loveless.

In his autobiography Connors writes about how, at Christmas time every year, Gloria would sing Big Jim a little jingle about wanting nothing for Christmas other than 'a gray cashmere sweater with a white fox collar'. That Gloria never got the sweater became a running family joke. One night in the early 1980s, by which time Big Jim had passed through that big toll booth in the sky, Jimmy paid his family a visit after yet another wildly successful but exhausting year spent mostly on the road. They all met up for dinner at Charlie Gitto's Italian Restaurant in downtown St Louis.

By then, of course, Jimmy was an enormous celebrity. Over dinner the family indulged in some domestic nostalgia, and they eventually started on the topic of the gray cashmere sweater. Gloria finally did get that sweater, in a nice box wrapped for Christmas, just a day or two later. It was a gift from a former St Louis mob boss named Shorty Caleca, by then a septuagenarian, who had overheard their conversation in Gitto's a few nights earlier. He gave Gloria what Big Jim never did.

Over the years, Jimmy Connors would do all he could to promote himself as a 'blue-collar' guy who embodied blue-collar earthiness – as if you couldn't be anything *but* vulgar if you were not to the manor born. But his collar probably was a lighter shade of blue than he ever realized. For it's hard to imagine that, with the status of John T. Connors in East St Louis, and Gloria Thompson Connors' history of hobnobbing with the suntanned and affluent tennis set, John Lennon had Jimmy Connors in mind when he wrote the song 'Working Class Hero'.

Yet Gloria Connors supported and fueled her son's conceit in that regard, even as her Jimmy became a great champion. After all, it dovetailed nicely with Gloria's insistence that the two of them were outsiders in the fancy-pants world of tennis. That theme only made it more natural for her to huddle with her boy, protecting, isolating, controlling, keeping him close as she worked out her terrible ambitions and unleashed revenge upon all the 'thems' of the world through the offices of Jimbo's unerring left hand and the chromed steel scimitar he brandished with it. And if that wasn't enough, his heart would prove to be steadfast and loyal.

*

Gloria and Two-Mom kneel on a seemingly flat but uneven stretch of concrete, meticulously following the markings they made as they paint white lines on what would ultimately become the tennis court in the backyard of the newly built home on 69th Street which the Connors moved into while Gloria was pregnant with Jimmy. Initially, the yard was filled with cinderblocks, discarded lumber and other construction debris — all of it surrounded by a tall, chain link fence. But a diligent cleanup left it looking like an orderly prison exercise yard.

It would be some time before Jimmy could join Johnny in hitting balls on that court, but Gloria wants to be prepared. In addition to the court, she finds two pieces of plywood and has them joined to create a backboard. There is nothing anything like this setup at a private house anywhere near 69th Street — or the entire neighborhood.

Jimmy is three and a half when he first picks up a racquet. But even the one Pop had cut down (there are no youth racquets yet) is still too heavy for the frail youngster. He's only able to lift it using both hands, so he begins to hit balls that way. Gloria notices that, surprisingly, her second son appears to be left-handed — he's the only person of that persuasion on either side of his family. Over time, Jimmy would drop his right hand off the racquet, but only on the forehand side.

Nobody of note at the time relied on a backhand hit with both hands on the handle; the closest well-known stroke was Ecuadorian champ Pancho Segura's lethal two-handed forehand. Gloria is unconcerned about her son's unorthodox backhand, and if she worries about how small and thin he is she keeps it to herself. She is, after all, the one who stands across the net from him every day once he's strong enough to hit the ball over, as well as the one who does her best to whack it right down his throat when she gets the opportunity.

Many years after she shaped Jimmy's game and attitude, Gloria would tell *Sports Illustrated*'s Frank Deford: 'We taught him to be a tiger. "Get those tiger juices flowing!" I would call out, and I told him to try and knock the ball down my throat, and he learned to do this because he found out that if I had the chance, I would knock it down his. Yes, sir. And then I would say, "You see, Jimbo, see what even your own mother will do to you on a tennis court?"'

But Gloria is no run-of-the-mill, driven parent/ coach. She has a great talent for getting into Johnny and Jimmy's minds (and that of anyone else she teaches) and, in Jimmy's own words, 'identify the right buttons to push'. Unlike many of her breed, Gloria doesn't believe in practicing her kids to death. Most of Jimmy's practices last for under an hour. On days when Jimmy is really playing well and eager to lose himself deeper and deeper in his communion with the ball, Gloria abruptly pulls the plug. 'That's enough for today.' Connors' practices rarely lasted more than forty-five minutes – a habit he would cling to throughout his career.

The rough surface and limited space at the sides and back of the court would ordinarily present an obstacle to playing and enjoying the game. But Gloria wasn't in this just for the fun of it. The bad bounce combined with the lack of adequate space helps create two of the most lethal aspects of Connors' mature game. The erratic rebound keeps him focused and on his toes, while the lack of space forces him to take the ball quickly after the bounce, while it is still on the rise. It is perhaps the most coveted – and most difficult to master – skill in the game.

Later, as the boys grow older, Gloria moves the practices to the more conventionally drawn courts at Jones Park, where the even, smooth courts allow the boys to keep the ball in play for longer periods. The courts at Jones Park feature nets made out of steel chain (partly so they could not be stolen), and the boys enjoy the loud tinkling they make when struck by a ball.

In the future many pundits and journalists would marvel at how Gloria and Two-Mom gave Jimmy a woman's game with which to beat men. The assessment is accurate. The game Gloria gives Jimmy, her game, is simple – and thus less prone to breakdown than some more elaborate styles. Gloria seems to know that in the hands of a sufficiently athletic, fleet, master of eye-hand coordination and timing, this 'woman's' game becomes any male opponent's worst nightmare. For men at this time, playing 'aggressively' means rushing forward to force the action at the net. For Connors, it means moving an opponent around mercilessly, driving up the pace (and, therefore, the risk) in the rallies, and finishing them off with bold placements when the geometry of the court allows.

The two most important ingredients in this game are preparation and footwork. Thus, during practice Gloria stands behind Jimmy, watching his every move. She is interested in the mechanics of his game, how well he moves the weight of his body into a shot, how quickly he moves his feet, how well prepared he is for an opponent's shot.

Usually, Pop Thompson tags along to watch practice as Two-Mom and Gloria work out the two boys. At first, he's prone to interject bits of advice culled from his own experience. But the icy looks he receives in unison from the two Thompson girls, mother and daughter, when he offers a tip persuade him that his talents would be better applied elsewhere. So he takes on the role of Jimmy's physical trainer, looking to prizefighters for his cues. He has Jimmy using the rope, running in heavy boots and carrying a weighted bag. The visible results of all this work are negligible. Jimmy remains a kind of stick figure.

*

The police car is weaving through traffic with a blaring horn, speeding. The driver is Johnny Connors, who isn't anywhere near legal driving age. He's not even a teenager. His kid brother Jimmy rides shotgun, while in the back Pop Thompson, still in a wet bathing suit, is holding a makeshift bandage to his forehead. It's split wide open, and he's bleeding like a stuck pig – the result of trying to teach Johnny and Jimmy a 'speed dive' in the shallow end of the swimming pool. The boys fear that if they don't get Pop to a hospital he will die. Pop will not die because he is a tough old bird.

Johnny and Jimmy are both expert drivers before they hit their teens thanks to the liberal lending policy Pop Thompson practices with his police car. It is, after all, city property. When Jimmy is just eight, he gets free driving lessons from Pop in Jones Park. When Pop stops by the house to visit with Gloria, the boys take the police car and drive to the store for some sodapop, or visit their friends. Astonished passers-by and fellow motorists sometimes see the two youngsters, their chins barely the height of the dashboard, and call the police. Pulled over, the boys just tell the policemen that they're the grandchildren of Al Thompson and the officers send them on their way, urging them to be careful driving back.

The automobile isn't the only form of locomotion Pop helps his grandsons master at an early age. He also teaches the boys how to hop the freight trains that run from the depot beyond the tennis courts in Jones Park. Sometimes the kids are still in their tennis whites while they run alongside the boxcar, grab a handhold and swing aboard. Once, they rode the rails as far as Kansas City, about 300 miles away. This becomes a cheap, fast form of local transportation for the Connors boys; they sometimes hop a railcar to get home from their grade school, St Phillip's.

But neither boy is fond of school. Jimmy, a frequent truant, will later describe it as 'torture'. The school has one advantage, and a decidedly non-blue collar one: a tennis court. Monsignor Forney, the headmaster, allows the Connors boys to play tennis during recess, and he occasionally hits with them. But in East St Louis the other kids predictably scoff at tennis as a 'sissy sport'. Jimmy is often teased and pushed around, especially when the sympathetic monsignor lets him leave school early to go play at Jones Park, even though Jimmy is merely in third grade. By then, though, Johnny is good with his fists and he looks after his runty brother.

Even after the beatings inflicted on Gloria and Pop, Big Jim takes the family to Jones Park and the boys feel safe, swimming in the pool, picnicking, fishing or rowing around the lake. When the boys are thirteen and eleven, they're besotted by Westerns and convince Big Jim to allow Johnny to use his savings from working at the toll booth to buy a quarter horse (it is an apt breed, given that Johnny was essentially buying it with quarters).

Surprisingly, Big Jim soon comes to share their interest in riding and before long buys his own horse, as well as one for Jimmy – the latter a palomino named Peaches. The boys occasionally take the horses and ride into the nearby hills to look for arrowheads and camp out overnight. But Jimmy quickly soured on playing Wild West. He prefers the creature comforts of his home. He prefers to stay close to Gloria, and tennis.

Jimmy plays his first sanctioned tournament when he is seven years old. Gloria drives Johnny and Jimmy to Flora for the Southern Illinois Championships, a regular stop on the midwestern junior circuit. Jimmy isn't ready to contend for titles yet; he's still small and short of power. But Johnny brings glory upon the family by winning the tournament as his younger brother looks on enviously. The image of a triumphant Johnny leaves a big impression on Jimmy; a year later he returns to Flora to claim the championship for himself. It is the first noteworthy win of his life.

The tennis courts are marked out on the waxed and highly polished floorboards of the Armory 138th Infantry, Missouri National Guard. Gloria and Jimmy feel like outsiders in this, the only indoor tennis facility in St Louis, the same venue where Arthur Ashe took great strides as a player as he developed and honed his volleying skills.

All other things aside, the discomfort the Connors feel here is understandable. The armory is the domain of the elite players from St Louis. This scrawny Connors boy, who is only eleven, and his omnipresent mother are interlopers, horning in on forbidden territory. Gloria finds a way around this; she offers to coach some of the kids if they in turn would hit with Jimmy if one of their number is a no-show, or turns up late.

In some instinctive way, Jimmy understands that his mother is offering herself for use by others in order for him to flourish. He will never forget this, even though at the time he lingers anxiously on the side lines, ever waiting on the off-chance that some kid will skip his allotted practice time, or be late enough for Jimmy to get out and hit a few balls.

Ultimately, Jimmy gets his fair share of tennis time at the armory and it plays an enormous part in his development. Playing on polished wood is like playing on ice; if you don't learn to attack and take the ball on the rise it's by you in the blink of an eye. The armory also enhances Jimmy's strengths – his quickness, reflexes and aggressive instincts. His ability on the surface only boosts his confidence, even as it drives another nail into the coffin of his brother John's interest. The incessant drumbeat of tennis, tennis, tennis and more tennis is getting to him.

Shortly after Gloria and Jimmy begin working out at the armory, Jimmy notices that Johnny often slips away from the training session at the first opportunity. When practice is finished, Jimmy is likely to find Johnny on the roof of the building, hurling crab apples at passing cars. There comes a day when Jimmy, patiently waiting for Gloria to finish teaching other kids – youths he has already sworn to demolish – hears Johnny call his name from the compound where the National Guard keeps its vehicles. Johnny has found a way to start one of the jeeps, and he urges Jimmy to jump in and go for a ride. That tour ends with Johnny slamming the jeep into a stationary National Guard truck, but the boys flee undetected.

Gloria sees the writing on the wall. Johnny is not only uninterested in becoming a tennis champion, his increasing delinquency suggests that he is in the throes of rebellion. This is something that concerns her in just one way: Jimmy adores Johnny, and it would be a disaster if she permitted Johnny's insurrectionist tendencies to rub off on his younger brother. In her mind, Johnny has crossed the Rubicon and – to hell with it. She tells Johnny to go ahead and do what he wants. Johnny appears fine with the situation. He goes on to join a delinquents' fight club in a damp and musty viaduct referred to by local youth, in the reverential tones reserved for such places, as 'the Rat's Hole'.

Gloria's position is based on an enormous leap of faith. Jimmy is still small, and only his exquisite timing compensates for his fundamental lack of muscle power. But Gloria knows it's time for her Jimbo to immerse himself in the world of tennis, head-on. He takes frequent beatings, many of them administered by boys a bit older but precociously strong and well-trained. She tries to temper Jimmy's disappointment by pointing out that he's just not 'big enough' yet, and assures him that if he keeps working hard and doing the right thing he will prevail.

Jimmy loves the competition, but he isn't wild about the social aspects of junior tennis. He bridles against rooming with his rivals, or having to sleep on the floor when a number of the kids are obliged to share a room. He makes his feelings known and Gloria begins to turn down offers of free housing (a tradition in cities that host national level tournaments). She says it's because the living conditions are unpredictable and sometimes inadequate, but other parents and coaches snipe that that Gloria Connors and her runty son think they're God's gift, or ambitious antisocial outsiders, aloof and uninterested in joining the community of junior tennis players.

The Orange Bowl tennis tournament, held at the end of every year in Miami, Fla., is a major junior event – the equal of the Grand Slam tournaments in prestige as well as the field it traditionally attracts. One afternoon during the 1964 edition of the tournament, Gloria and Jimmy are walking by the practice courts when they notice that a small crowd has gathered to watch the action on a nearby court.

Curious, the Connors' group moseys over to see what the hubbub is all about. Jimmy can immediately see the sun flashing on the chromed steel of what appears to be some kind of tennis racquet, and he can hear the distinct sound the ball makes as it comes off the strings of this instrument. A shot coming off a standard, gut-strung wooden racquet makes a crisp pop, not unlike that of a champagne cork coming free. This sound is like that, but it's muffled. It sounds almost like a thump.

Jimmy regards the racquet. It's chromium-bright, with two rails extending from the plastic and leather handle to form a 'V' into which is nestled the round head of the racquet. The head isn't formed of laminated wood with closely spaced holes drilled all around it to accommodate strings. This head is more or less oval, with a framework of steel wire into which the strings are laced. It's the same idea as a backyard trampoline secured to a steel frame with a network of springs. It also produces a similar effect.

This racquet is a prototype of the Wilson T-2000, and Jimmy immediately falls head over heels in love with it. In his twelve-year-old's eyes, it is Excalibur. And he isn't even obliged to draw it out of a stone. Gloria knows Jack Staton, the Wilson representative who is putting on the demonstration. She asks Staton if Jimmy can try a frame and he promises to get him one as soon as the racquet goes into production. Racquet makers like to build relationships with promising junior players, and that often translates into long-term brand loyalty.

A few weeks later, a package addressed to Jimmy arrives at his home. It contains four brand spanking new T-2000s, with a friendly note from Staton. Two-Mom is skeptical of these newfangled steel racquets; heck, there aren't even any holes in the frame so that she and Pop can string the things the traditional way, using an awl and a pick. The racquet has to be laced somehow, almost like a shoe.

It takes the grandparents a while to figure out how to string the racquet, after which Gloria and Jimmy dash out to test it. When Jimmy hits the first ball, the entire racquet seems to explode in his hand because it is so flexible, and the trampoline effect sends vibrations right down to the handle (there being no wood to absorb the shock). The ball flies over the fence. Gloria and Jimmy keep at it, and by the end of the afternoon the boy can keep most of his shots in play. But every once in a while, when he catches the ball on the perfect spot on the face of the racquet, it flies like a rifle shot. Jimmy can sense that he's holding an assassin's tool, the one he wants to use to do his own special brand of wet work.

At first, Jimmy loses numerous matches because of how hard it is to control the racquet. Other tennis people ogle the thing with skepticism when he shows up at tournaments with the Wilson racquet. But over time, a few other kids (and a number of adults, including Billie Jean King and fellow American Clark Graebner) try out the racquet. Jimmy revels in the frustration they feel trying to tame the steel racquet. He knows that the adjustment period is a lot longer than they hoped or imagined, and that the payoff for sticking with it is much greater than they envisioned.

Gradually, Jimmy masters the explosive steel frame even if it still produces the odd unexpected flier. In general, it gives all of his shots a lot more pop because the racquet can be strung tighter (and thus produce more power) than wood frames. The open-throat configuration (at the time, most wooden racquets had a solid shaft and neck that widened out to merge with the head) enables him to generate greater racquet-head speed. And the T-2000 frame looks so freaking unbelievably cool that the confidence it gives him is worth a few points per set, easy.

To some, the T-2000 is a travesty — a plug-ugly tool that cannot be compared to a lovingly crafted wood racquet, with its multiple laminations (often of different, contrasting species of wood), artistic inlays and glossy varnished finish. Some tennis insiders consider the T-2000 a typically *American* innovation — practical, easy and cheap to manufacture and maintain (unlike a wood racquet, the Wilson steel will not warp; thus it requires no racquet press), reasonable in price, and utterly lacking in aesthetic touches or appeal.

Unbeknownst to some of the critics, the T-2000 was the brainchild of the legendary French player René Lacoste, who patented it in 1953 and licensed the manufacturing of the frame to Wilson for the US market.

The mounting cost of travel and related expenses puts the squeeze on Gloria's budget. She can no longer swing the cost with the lessons she gives at the armory. She finds a job teaching tennis at a club in Forest Park, St Louis. Her employer, knowing that Gloria is deeply immersed in Jimmy's junior career, is understanding. He allows her ample time off to travel with her son.

Between 1963 and 1967 Gloria and Two-Mom hustle Jimmy to the Manker Patten Tennis Club, in Chattanooga, Tennessee, to take part in twelve-and-under and fourteen-and-under junior championships. Each year, they are disappointed when Jimmy comes up against the best players. The reality is that Jimmy cannot even beat his mother – never mind the best young men in the land. But that changes when Jimmy is fifteen years old.

Gloria and Jimmy travel to Kalamazoo, Michigan, for the boys' sixteen and under national championships. He is playing yet another practice set with Gloria, now swinging that T-2000 like the hammer of Thor. But Gloria, being Gloria, won't give an inch. The set is agonizingly close, and eventually Jimmy arrives at a set point. Gloria gambles and approaches the net during the next point and Jimmy hits a crisp, pinpoint passing shot. The next thing, he is running to the net, tears welling in his eyes, 'I'm sorry! I'm sorry!'

Gloria smiles. She too is fighting back tears. Many years later she would tell writer Frank Deford that she said, 'No, no, Jimmy, don't you know? This is one of the happiest days of my life.' She added, 'Now I know it's time to move on.'

Not coincidentally, a few days later Jimmy wins the title at Kalamazoo. He is the official national champion in his age group. Gloria is already planning their next move. They will go from the gray, semi-industrial maze of suburban St Louis, with its cold and drafty armory and empty park benches and autumn-naked hardwoods, to the sunny environs she reluctantly left some eighteen years earlier. Back then, she was an obedient daughter coming to grips with her duty to return home to East St Louis, to meet what could not have seemed like an altogether promising fate.

Gloria will be returning to California with that fate in tow. The woman Pauline Betz had described as 'the sweetest, most ingenuous, lovely person' had been hardened by what life as a mother and wife had to offer, but she had also been rewarded with a great gift. And she knows exactly whom to show it to, and offer it to, when she returns to Los Angeles.

CHAPTER THREE

Joe College

'The word "undemonstrative" is correct. But inside, Arthur had emotions. You know, he had enormous emotions. One of the things that always pissed me off about Arthur is that he would just not let them out. I sometimes would try intentionally to get him mad, just to get a reaction out of him. But no. With him it was always, "It's no big deal . . . that's okay . . ."

Even later, when he was suffering from AIDS, I would try to get stuff out of him over the phone and it was always, "I'm okay . . . my blood is okay . . ." like that. I just never saw Arthur blow up.'

Charlie Pasarell, childhood rival and close
lifelong friend of Ashe

Arthur Ashe is nervous. He sits in the fancy Los Angeles restaurant, to the left of the University of California, Los Angeles (UCLA) tennis head coach J.D. Morgan. To Morgan's right sits Charlie Pasarell, the US junior champion and a youth who first met Ashe at the Orange

Bowl junior championships in 1956. On that occasion, they played the quarter-finals and Pasarell won.

Still, the two kids struck up a lasting friendship that transcended their rivalry. Charlie used to wonder why, at junior events, Arthur wasn't often out goofing around and playing with the other youngsters in their spare time. Later, he realized it was because Arthur was being protected by whomever was his chaperone on that occasion. He was being protected because of the delicate situation created by his race.

At this time, the United States and Australia are the titans of tennis. And in the US, the path to glory at Wimbledon, Forest Hills and in Davis Cup competition runs through the universities of the nation. America's four-year colleges have robust athletic programs that act as four-year developmental platforms for the finest young athletes in almost all sports. Top-flight educational institutions, both private (like the University of Southern California, or Notre Dame University) and state supported (like UCLA, or Michigan State University) value and support their athletic programs as robustly as institutions better known for their sports teams than their academic clout. The colleges compete to attract the most talented recruits, who get a 'free ride' (slang for a full scholarship) in return for the work they do to boost the visibility and reputation of the schools for whom they labor. The only outstanding exception is the Ivy League institutions (like Harvard and Princeton), which do not offer athletic scholarships but also welcome gifted athletes who wish to attend those prestigious colleges.

It says something about the status of tennis in California in the early 1960s that Morgan, who would go on to national prominence as the athletic director of UCLA (under his direction, UCLA would win thirty national titles in a host of sports ranging from water polo to basketball), is the coach of the tennis team. Recruiting talent is part of his job, and Pasarell and Ashe are perhaps the two most coveted recruits for the class entering college in 1962 (the class of '66).

Pasarell, the scion of a distinguished Puerto Rican family, made his debut at the US Open (then the US National Championships, from which professional players were still barred) as a sixteen-year-old in 1960. Ashe played his first US Nationals at the same age, albeit a year earlier, losing in the first round to Rod Laver. He threw up before that match, but discreetly, into his towel.

Pasarell and Ashe liked the idea of going to the same college, and both liked the idea of California. But they were undecided between the University of Southern California (USC) and UCLA, both of which had excellent tennis programs.

On his visit to UCLA, Ashe is enthralled by the pretty environment in which the campus is located, in Westwood. It's sunny, clean, warm and inviting. Ever since he left Richmond to finish school and develop his game in St Louis he could be described as homeless – or, to put it in a more acceptable light, a footloose man of the world.

And now here he is, sitting with the head tennis coach of the UCLA Bruins (the state flag of California has a bear on it), lost in the wonder of it all for a few precious moments before he feels Morgan's left hand clasp his forearm as it rests on the table and sees, from the corner of his eye, that the coach's right hand is similarly locked on to Charlie's right forearm. An imposing figure to begin with, Morgan has a deep, gravelly voice. He declares: 'It's good to have both of you as Bruins.'

Charlie shoots Arthur a glance. Arthur looks a little sheepish, but keeps his mouth shut. Neither of them has decided upon UCLA; in fact, they have yet to visit USC. Neither of them wants to rush into a decision. Neither of them knows just what benefits his scholarship offers. Neither of them has the courage to point any of this out to Morgan.

It's official. Charlie Pasarell and Arthur Ashe are UCLA Bruins.

The bookworm Arthur Ashe Jr has always been interested in architecture, but the potential Wimbledon champion knows that the academic demands for a major in that discipline would be rigorous – considerably more rigorous than choosing the vague and less demanding study of Business Administration. So he takes the path of least resistance, the one that also will allow him the most time to work on his game.

The year Ashe spent in St Louis as a high school senior was challenging in many ways. But it was enormously productive in one key area, He arrived in St Louis as a 'pusher', a player who stays in the back court, near the baseline, and strives to keep the ball in play. But in St Louis, exposed to aggressive serve-and-volley players who often practiced on the slick wooden floor of the armory, he discovered his penchant for the risky, attacking game that paid such dividends on fast surfaces – most notably grass, most super-notably the slick grass courts of Forest Hills (where the US National championships were played) and Wimbledon.

By the time he arrives at UCLA, Ashe is bold to the point of seeming almost 'reckless'. The conditions and competition in St Louis undoubtedly had much to do with this transformation, but it also seems that Ashe was in some ways liberated when he left the familiar environs of Richmond. As a player, he had the opportunity to reinvent himself without having to worry about pleasing either of the Johnsons, Ron Charity, or anyone else.

Ashe's first roommate at UCLA is fellow tennis player David Reed. But, as a sophomore, Ashe moves in with Pasarell and, for a brief period, a Haitian team-mate, Jean Edouard Baker. When Baker moves on, Ashe and Pasarell remain roommates for about three years, until Ashe graduates in 1966.

The two young men live the carefree lives of privileged elite athletes. They are both responsible and dedicated to their tennis, but the definition of training at that time is a far cry from what it will become as the game explodes globally. The tennis players are obliged to practice only on weekdays, leaving their weekends free.

The most revered athletes at UCLA are the stars of a basketball squad that would win a nearly incomprehensible ten national championships in twelve years, despite the fact that the title is decided, much like a tennis tournament, by a straightforward single-elimination tournament with a draw of sixty-eight teams/schools. Before tennis practice, Ashe and Pasarell often shoot baskets with the likes of Walt Hazzard, Gail Goodrich and Fred Slaughter, all of whom would become celebrated players in the UCLA basketball dynasty. Sometimes one or more of these men room with Ashe and Pasarell, who like to cook for each other and enjoy throwing parties.

It is after a dorm dance during his sophomore year that Ashe finally gets up the nerve to do something he had resolved to do long before: ask a white girl out on a date. When he took the plunge, he was somewhat disappointed to discover that she wasn't even a UCLA student, but a pretty dental assistant. Worse yet, she was utterly blasé about what, in Ashe's conservative mind, was a barrier-busting occasion that had caused sweat to break out on his palms.

But even in the liberal, sophisticated precincts of Southern California, where the rebellion against the putative bland and squeaky clean 1950s was already beginning, the stinger of racial prejudice had not been excised. Each year, one of the posh clubs down around Newport Beach would invite the UCLA tennis team to take part in a tournament and social gathering. But when Ashe is on the team, the club asks that the team leave him behind. J.D. Morgan says 'absolutely not', and he keeps the entire UCLA squad home.

It's counter-intuitive, especially in an era marked by a heighted state of racial consciousness, but Pasarell and others are only vaguely aware of such things, and basically unconcerned with them. They, including Ashe, are healthy and virile young men who feel a powerful, natural bond with each other, so they shrug such things off unless they are forced to grapple with them. Ashe's attitude absolves them of that chore. Years later Pasarell will tell me, 'This is the great thing about Arthur: he never made an issue out of it [racism]. You know, he was, like, "Okay. So what? They don't want me down there." That's the way he was. Just deals with it.'

Still, Pasarell takes note when he pledges for the Beta Theta, Phi fraternity, but Ashe abstains and later goes off to pledge for a 'black' fraternity based off campus. When Pasarell attends a party at Ashe's fraternity, it sinks in that in many ways there is a real and deep if rarely discussed divide between black and white in America.

Ashe himself is accustomed to spontaneous eruptions of racism; he has experienced them all his life, although in some ways it was easier to manage in Richmond, where at least he needn't fine-tune his radar for hypocrisy. At UCLA he also comes face-to-face with the black nationalist movement and he engages in a long conversation on race with Ron Karenga who, in his drive to instill an appreciation of African culture in American blacks, will come up with the idea of a holiday called 'Kwanzaa'. But Ashe does not respond well to heated or confrontational rhetoric. By nature, he is contemplative and rational. By cultural bequest he is a Southern gentleman.

Ashe is also the object of great admiration, and he receives support, sometimes from unexpected sources. While sophomores, Ashe and Pasarell are invited to the Rancho Club, not far from Westwood. Established institutions like the Los Angeles Tennis Club, at the time, did not particularly welcome Jews or show business personalities (never mind blacks). Consequently, those segments of LA society formed clubs of their own, like the Rancho Club or the Beverly Hills Tennis Club, in response to the anti-Semitism and general snobbery that were often as pervasive as outright racism – even in those rarefied social circles.

This is a lark for the boys. They know it's an opportunity to show off their polished games, as well as the cute tushies they jam into their 'tighty-whitey' tennis shorts. And then there's the lavish country club lunch. All goes as expected, and during lunch one of the presiding matrons asks if the boys are going to play at Wimbledon in a few months' time. Pasarell volunteers that he will play the NCAA championships and then go try his hand at Wimbledon.

When the lady asks Ashe his plans, he admits he has none beyond the NCAAs. When pressed, he reveals that he just can't afford the trip to London. Whereupon the lady begins to make the rounds of all the folks having lunch, holding up this one for a hundred dollars, shaming that one into kicking in three hundred. Within minutes, she returns to where Arthur and Charlie are seated and presents Ashe with her take, which Pasarell later judges to be between seven hundred and a thousand dollars. Ashe is so stunned he can barely mumble his thanks.

It's a pattern that will mark Ashe's development right up through his early years as a professional. He's never just another tennis player. Sometimes, he's a symbol of his society's most benighted prejudices, at other times the beneficiary of touching acts of support. He brings out the worst in certain institutions, and the best in some people. He's spent his early years being told he's 'too black', but soon he will, in the opinion of some, be 'too white'. He will be many things to many people, but the one thing he will not be is plain old tennis genius Arthur Ashe.

Already, Ashe knows he will have to deal with the power and interplay of these forces, but this isn't the time yet. His life is accelerating like a fast car on a long, straight stretch of road, and the incidents of discrimination and callous insensitivity as well as the displays of faith and support, are just flying by. They are mile markers that will be there for the duration of his journey.

Arthur turns out to be an ideal roommate in the one-bedroom apartment he shares with Pasarell. He's neat and orderly; he does his share of the chores without prodding. But Pasarell notices something odd about his friend: his sleeping habits.

The men have their beds against the wall on either side of the room, and it seems that Arthur never needs to make his, while Charlie's was often a mess. It seems Arthur would just slide under the sheets, pull them up to his chin and fall asleep.

Sometimes, Charlie wakes in the middle of the night and he looks over to where Arthur is sleeping. He's still there all right; in fact, it looks like he hasn't moved. This is a little spooky. Charlie thinks, 'He looks like a mummy.' Then, in a moment of dark humor, he wonders if Arthur is even still alive.

Come morning, Arthur invariably slides out from between the sheets as delicately as he slipped in the previous night. The vacant bed sits there, unmussed, while at his own bed Charlie tugs at the corners of the sheets and beats the pillow back into acceptable shape.

At this time, the USC Trojans are UCLA's arch rival in National Collegiate Athletic Association (NCAA) sports. When Ashe and Pasarell arrive at UCLA the Trojans, led by Dennis Ralston (who would go on to play a Wimbledon final), are particularly strong. Morgan's Bruins are soundly thrashed in the 1963 finals, and they must travel the following year along with everyone else, to play at Michigan State University, in East Lansing, Mich.

Morgan's two young stars are no longer skittish freshmen; they each have a year of seasoning. The coach has high hopes for a good tournament in East Lansing, but first he and the team must get there – and Morgan hates flying. He has a brainstorm: he will send the bulk of the team to Michigan via commercial jet, while he drives all the way from Los Angeles, taking along Ashe and Pasarell.

Morgan and his two charges leave a week before everyone else, and Pasarell will remember it as one of the greatest trips of his life. It is just the three of them, and Oklahoman Morgan is happy to open their eyes, the eyes of blinkered tennis savants, to the wonders of the country landscape. He alerts them to a herd of antelope not far off the road, and the boys will obediently take note. Morgan is good at judging time and distances. His voice rumbles as he says something like, 'In exactly two hours and thirty-seven minutes we're going to stop in this little town that has a beautiful park and get some watermelon, because they have the best watermelon!'

Arthur and Charlie just exchange glances. Town? Where? This is the middle of Wyoming and how does Coach know there's great watermelon here? But almost exactly two hours and thirty-seven minutes later, the trio is sitting in a pretty little park, eating as fine an example of watermelon as either boy has tasted.

Occasionally, Morgan abruptly pulls over on a quiet little country road. He tells the boys, 'We're going to do a little work now.' The boys get out and begin to jog while Morgan paces them in the car. When Morgan decides they have run enough, he pulls the car over and they clamber back inside.

Pasarell still has vivid memories of that trip; he calls it a 'fantastic' experience. Unfortunately for Morgan, USC once again dominates the NCAAs, with Dennis Ralston retaining his singles title. Ashe and Pasarell will have to wait, but not for long. As a junior in 1965, Ashe would lead UCLA to the NCAA team championship, and win the individual singles title. USC would get the team title back the following year, but Pasarell would win the prestigious singles title.

*

There is no end to the tennis available to an eager, gifted player in Southern California. While Arthur and Charlie are still at UCLA, Pancho Segura invites them down to play as guests at the Beverly Hills Tennis Club. He books a lesson for Ashe, but when the young player forks out the $15 fee for the lesson Segura surreptitiously returns $10 into Ashe's palm. Having grown up brown and dirt-poor in Guayaquil, Ecuador, Segura feels a natural affinity with the lean, poised, African American youngster (both were suspected of having suffered from rickets; in Segura's case it was true), even though his job now consists mostly of servicing the tepid athletic needs of Los Angeles's Jewish aristocracy.

But there they are, Arthur and Charlie, hobnobbing with the likes of Dinah Shore and Charlton Heston, just a couple of college kids hitting balls on the same courts where Segura some years later would put the final, vital finishing touches on the game of Jimmy Connors.

Despite what fate has in store, Segura is particularly supportive of Ashe, whom he sees as a fellow 'brown body' in a world dominated by handsomely tanned white ones. So he also arranges for Arthur and Charlie to teach in a Pasadena, Ca., tennis program funded by the family of Cathy Lee Crosby, a woman who had ranked as high as no. 7 in US tennis but who was better known for her role as a co-host for the popular American television show of the 1980s *That's Incredible*.

This program plays a shaping role in the careers of two other outstanding players, two-time Grand Slam champion Stan Smith (a local Pasadena boy) and Tom Leonard. Sometimes, they are on the same court as Arthur and Charlie, and even Segura. He comes up as a special coach and each of the kids on the development team gets to hit with the old master.

The payment for the boys on those Saturday mornings in Pasadena is about $4.50, but they don't mind. They get to play with the best local youngsters as well as other top players, like another Segura recruit Allen Fox. The money is enough to stake Charlie and Arthur to an excellent deli sandwich and a movie later that afternoon.

The local tournaments in that neck of the woods bring out a host of blue-chip players. Stan Smith, who will become another of Ashe's closest friends, recalls one in particular, at the Valley Hunt Club in Pasadena. At the time Smith, who is four years younger than Ashe, is still in high school and awed by the quality of the players by whom he is surrounded.

Pasarell knows that his roommate Ashe tends to zone out when he is about to engage in high-stakes competition. He will more or less disappear, going off on his own to watch a movie, or peruse a book store – presumably to relax and feel no obligation to socialize when he has bigger things on his mind. This tournament features USC's most accomplished player, Dennis Ralston. He is on a collision course in the draw with Ashe, and the brackets hold up: the semi-finals are Ashe vs Ralston and Pasarell vs yet another of the outstanding players who will leave a mark on the game, Tom Edelfsen.

On the morning of their match, Charlie drives Arthur to the club in his little red Ford Falcon. When he pops the trunk of his car, he just groans. Arthur has forgotten to bring his racquets. Again. It is a curious, unconscious oversight, and one that trails Ashe through-out his life. Perhaps it's best to think of it as Ashe's special gift to the armchair psychiatrist community.

Ashe is not a fan of Pasarell's racquets; among other things, the grips are too fat to suit him. Dave Reed, another team-mate, is also on hand, and Arthur corners him and sheepishly asks, 'Can I borrow one of your racquets? I have to play Dennis.'

At the time, almost every player on the planet is using the Wilson Jack Kramer racquet; it's so ubiquitous that the players have to mark the frames with their initials to be able to tell which is whose when they're leaned against a bench or the net.

Soon the matches are underway on adjacent courts. After about an hour, Pasarell sees that Ashe has won the first set and they're well into the second. Ralston is unhappy – a condition that anyone who knows scowling, short-fused Dennis Ralston thinks of as his default mode. Ralson has popped a string on one of his three racquets and, after having lost the set, he smashed another racquet to smithereens on the net post. Now

Ashe and Ralston are walking around as if they're looking for someone's lost car keys. Ralston is muttering and gesticulating, Ashe looks perplexed.

Finally, Ralston and Ashe are in conference at the net, looking at Ashe's — or, rather, Dave Reed's — racquet. Suddenly, the player is no longer just Arthur Ashe, he's positively ashen. Reed plays with the same Jack Kramer autograph racquet as Ralston. They share the initials, DR. The players quickly do the math and come to the same serio-comic conclusion: Ashe had inadvertently picked up Ralston's last racquet. He's been beating the pants off Dennis Ralston, the last guy anyone would want to piss off, with the man's own racquet.

'Jeez, Dennis,' Ashe says in a small voice. 'I'm sorry.'

Fuming, Ralston yanks his racquet out of Ashe's hand. But the damage is done. Ralston is seeing red, and he's also stupefied, a combination that does not bode well. Ashe goes on to finish him off with no further controversy.

Back in the locker room, Pasarell looks on, trying to suppress his laughter, as Ralston takes that third and final racquet — the one Ashe had been using so artfully for so much of the match — and smashes it into tiny bits on a steel post. Ralston had arrived that morning at the Valley Hunt Club with high hopes and three racquets. He leaves stunned and empty-handed.

*

This hothouse atmosphere makes everyone a better player. The sheer number of gifted, accomplished players in the Los Angeles area is nothing short of amazing. The seemingly endless practice sessions, the matches, the blisters, the anecdotes, the laughs, the challenges and the tears and triumphs blend into each other in a succession of days so uniformly glorious that they seem as one. It's good to be in college. It's good to be enormously talented and arcing upward toward that warm California sun, surrounded and tested and invariably made better, stronger, by a legion of like-minded peers.

At the same time, Arthur Ashe enjoys the intellectual stimulation of college. His disciplined mind is also receiving rigorous workouts, some of which make him uncomfortable. The Black Power movement is stirring to life, and while Ashe stubbornly refuses to immerse himself in racial preoccupations, some of the questions materializing from the ether of a changing society are vexing ones. He isn't demonstrative, he isn't angry, he doesn't believe in the politics of confrontation any more than he believes in some essential right to be rude. It just isn't his style. He isn't consumed by his tennis ambitions or results, either, and in some ways this makes it easier for him.

Occasionally, the phone rings in Charlie or Arthur's apartment and, upon picking it up, whoever answers recognizes the voice of that champion who is revered and feared in equal measures, Pancho Gonzalez. He simply growls into the receiver: 'LA Tennis Club, two thirty.'

If Arthur or Charlie tries to beg off, citing the need to study for an anthropology test – or something Gonzalez deems equally foolish – he merely listens to the protest patiently and then repeats what sounds suspiciously like a warning, and in a slightly more commanding tone: 'LA Tennis Club. Two thirty.'

The youngsters hustle to gather their tennis kits and scramble to find a classmate willing to take and later share the anthropology class notes.

Gonzalez, who is of Mexican descent, is the alpha dog, and nobody has the gumption to challenge his authority. And everyone knew it. When Pancho dispensed advice, the players digested it – even on those occasions when they might have been better served by politely declining the serving.

Pasarell never forgets that, on occasion, Pancho tells his attentive acolytes that they must be like the ancient Incas – guys who can 'go running through mountains for a hundred miles or more without drinking water'. Gonzalez's message? Don't drink too much water.

Allen Fox, a brilliant student with a scientific mind as well as the NCAA singles champion in 1961, sometimes goes nuts when Gonzalez trots out one of his theories – none of which is based on anything more empirical than Gonzalez's own convictions, although the titan does stop short of recommending the application of leeches. The two men engage in heated arguments that go round and round, neither man giving an inch, Fox growing increasingly frustrated because down deep he knows better than to get sucked into a debate with an imperious warrior cursed with the pride of Achilles and blessed with a head as thick as the wall of a typical Mexican adobe dwelling.

The acolytes mostly listen. They don't know who to believe about this water stuff. Allen Fox is a smart guy and a helluva good player and debater. Pancho Gonzalez is a charismatic living legend — a tennis deity. They decide they're not that thirsty anyway.

Unbeknownst to their parents, Charlie and Arthur both buy motorcycles while they are at UCLA. Charlie's is an old, small Honda, but Arthur uncharacteristically goes big. He buys a giant white land yacht — not a Harley-Davidson, but the details have been lost in time — from its previous owner, UCLA team-mate and friend Larry Nagler.

Arthur allows Charlie to ride it now and again, but it's so huge, and such a growling, vibrating, powerful machine that it actually scares him. Charlie is convinced that Arthur is going to kill himself on the beast, and he feels a surge of relief when Arthur finally gets rid of it.

Neither of the friends is obliged to wait too much longer for adequate transportation. During their college careers (Charlie will stay on at UCLA for a year after Arthur graduates in 1966), both men are named to the US Davis Cup team. It's a high honor for two kids with rapidly maturing tennis games and strong patriotic feelings. But the most welcome, immediate outcome is that they are now paid $28 a day. The stipend accrues on a daily basis, even if the players are merely practicing at home. In effect, they have become salaried employees of the USLTA, their full-time job consisting of playing tennis and showing up to represent the US in sporadic Davis Cup ties.

Pasarell immediately goes out and buys himself a snappy Chevy Camaro, and Ashe chooses a sleek Ford Thunderbird. Can it get much better than this?

Yes, it can, and soon enough, it does.

In September 1963, while still just a sophomore at UCLA, Ashe is selected for a Davis Cup tie, an 'America zone' final against Venezuela. He is the first African American man chosen for the competition. At the time, the Davis Cup still follows the 'Challenge Round' model, with the champion nation defending its title against the last nation standing after a year-long global play-offs. In the Davis Cup lexicon, a match between two nations is a 'tie' and each of the matches in the best-of-five tie is called a 'rubber'.

Against Venezuela, Dennis Ralston and Marty Riessen win the first two singles rubbers, and they combine to win the doubles rubber as well. With the tie clinched for the US, Ashe is inserted to play the fourth match, a 'dead rubber'. He wins it easily, but the talent available to US coach Bob Kelleher is such that Ashe isn't selected to play again until mid-1965.

In the interim, Ashe's game continues to develop. In the spring of 1965, Ashe wins the NCAA singles title – again, he is the first African American to make the breakthrough (Ashe's win in both singles and doubles, with Ian Crookenden of New Zealand, helps seal the team win for UCLA over hated rival USC). Later in June, Ashe easily wins two matches in an Americas zone semi-final against overmatched Canada.

Three months later, Ashe is selected to play in the Davis Cup zonal final against Mexico. The other singles player on the team that meets Mexico on a hard court in Dallas is Dennis Ralston, who has long since replaced those Wilson Jack Kramer autograph racquets he smashed up after losing to Ashe back in Pasadena.

Ashe and Ralston win their singles matches on the opening day, but the Mexican team of Rafael Osuna and Tony Palafox take the doubles. With the US leading 2-1, Ashe plays the fourth rubber and clinches the tie for the US with a convincing win over Palafox. The result gives Ashe a bracing shot of confidence as the US National Championships approaches.

In August 1965, while Ashe is still in his junior year at UCLA, he further impresses the cognoscenti at the tournament that will brand him a future star: the US

National Championships, second in prestige only to Wimbledon. The tournament game is still for amateurs only; top professionals like Rod Laver, Pancho Gonzalez, Ken Rosewall and many others are still barred from playing in Grand Slam events. They barnstorm around the nation, playing one-night stands and other exhibitions. But the momentum is building to reverse that long-standing separation of amateurs and pros.

Twenty-two years old, Ashe has already logged six US Nationals. His best previous result was in 1964, when he beat two players who will enjoy long and satisfying pro careers, Tom Okker and Marty Riessen. But Ashe was stopped in the fourth round that year, the loser of an epic five-set clash with one of the great Australian players, Tony Roche.

A year later, Ashe slashes his way to the quarter-finals without the loss of a set. There he meets defending champion Roy Emerson, fresh off yet another big win – at Wimbledon. Emerson is well on his way to a career haul of eleven Grand Slam titles (a record that will stand until Pete Sampras shatters it some thirty years later, albeit with some caveats pertaining to the long absence of pros like Rod Laver and Pancho Gonzalez from the Grand Slam mix). Ashe finally loses a set at the US championships, but he goes on to upset 'Emmo' in four sets, 13-11, 6-4, 10-12, 6-2.

The win dispels what doubt any open-minded person might have had about Ashe's potential as a

Grand Slam contender. There are those who are still skeptical because of the color of Ashe's skin; they think 'Negroes' are intrinsically too lazy, and perhaps too emotionally volatile, to excel at a game that, at the highest level, requires a tremendous amount of sheer physical zeal (as demonstrated by the importance of good footwork), sustained mental discipline and emotional self-control.

Ashe has developed from a baseliner into a swash-buckling attacker who sometimes eschews the safe shot and goes for broke just for the hell of it. He likes to try the ridiculously difficult shot, even in a tight spot, because it's fun. Some see this as a shortcoming, rather than a willingness that adds an additional dimension to a game already supercharged with power in the form of Ashe's great cannonball serve and stinging backhand.

Ashe never loses his cool; he never smashes a ball into the backstop in frustration, or glares at a line judge by whom he feels wronged. That lesson drilled into him so many years ago by his father on that hot asphalt court in Richmond is burned into his psyche – much as the timing and mechanics of that gorgeous backhand ('I would win everything if I had that backhand', his pal Pasarell would say) are burned into muscle memory. About the only valid criticism of Ashe is that, at times, he is subject to a loss of concentration, or perhaps it's inspiration. As the Aussies like to say, 'he goes walkabout'. For the doubters, that will have to do.

Match-by-match, round-by-round, Ashe is proving the critics wrong wherever he plays and winning admirers. He has a wonderful, compact game that is as elegant as it is explosive. He is a model of sportsmanship and composure. The Black Power movement is gaining steam on campuses around the nation, and Ashe himself is working up the determination to abandon his stance as a bystander and speak out for his people. Yet at the same time he won't renounce his country. He feels the tug of patriotism and admits to getting goose bumps when he hears the chair umpire at a typical Davis Cup tie call out, 'Game, set, and match – United States'. Not 'Arthur Ashe' but 'United States'.

While at UCLA, Ashe has been enrolled in Army ROTC (Reserve Officer Training Corps). This is a program in which the government contributes heavily to the education of a participant, in exchange for which he or she agrees to take a number of military courses and summer training programs while in college, and to serve in active or reserve duty for a specific period after graduation.

Ashe has tried numerous times to coax Pasarell into joining him in ROTC, but Pasarell never understood the logic behind it. They were already at college on athletic scholarships, he would argue. The Vietnam war was in full swing at this time. ROTC students were making a commitment to serve, but they also knew they were not subject to conscription. The draftee had no control over his own fate; if called, he swiftly found himself in the army, shipping out to fight as a foot soldier in Southeast Asia. As an ROTC candidate and outstanding tennis player, Ashe was unlikely ever to see combat duty. But he undoubtedly felt patriotic obligations - not least because his own brother Johnnie had cast his lot with the United States Marine Corps. He would serve two tours of duty in Vietnam and take two bullets, neither of them fatal nor crippling, for his country.

Ashe is ready to venture forth into the world. He knows that upon graduation in June 1966 he will enter the United States Army. He does not know that he will spend most of his active duty at the US military academy at West Point, working as a 'data processor' while also acting as the head of the army tennis program.

Ashe is obliged to miss Wimbledon in 1968 because of his military commitments. He sees, on the first day of play in London, that his friend and roommate Charlie Pasarell has pulled off an astonishing first-round defeat of defending champion Manuel Santana. Ashe sends his pal a congratulatory telegram. The college roommates would remain fast friends, and continue to show their support for each other in numerous ways. One of those ways was utterly inadvertent but ultimately of critical value to Ashe and his legacy.

In September 1971, when Pancho Gonzalez was forty-three years old, he made it to the final of what was then, arguably, the second best American tournament, the Pacific Southwest Championships (Los Angeles).

Gonzalez's opponent was nineteen-year old Jimmy Connors, who was having the same kind of year Arthur Ashe had enjoyed in 1965. Prior to meeting Gonzalez, Connors had just recorded what would be his own career breakthrough win, his foil the same man who had helped launch Ashe to fame at the 1965 US Open, Roy Emerson.

Pasarell watches the final of that 1971 PSW tournament in awe – so much so that years later he would still remember individual points as if they were being played out right before his eyes. The only way to describe what Gonzalez is doing doesn't really fit the theme, which is that of a forty-three-year-old icon with the heart of a lion grappling with a rangy, mobile, viciously competitive teenager who revels in humiliating his rivals.

Suprising everyone, glowering, explosive, Gonzalez plays a 'soft' game, using touch and judicious placement to confuse and flummox Connors as he records one for the lore and legend of the game, winning 3-6, 6-3, 6-3.

Pasarell is mature enough to know exactly what he has just witnessed: 'The greatest tennis lesson I've ever seen somebody give.'

Pasarell files away the experience. It will come in handy, but not for him.

CHAPTER FOUR

Jimbo and Segu

'I am not making this up. That first day at the Beverly Hills Tennis Club, my father came off the court after hitting with Jimmy for less than twenty minutes and he said: "This guy is going to be the next champion of the world."'

Spencer Segura, son of Pancho Segura and
long-time friend of Jimmy Connors

It's the mid-1940s and Gloria Thompson is living the most carefree days of her life. She's playing tennis, traveling and meeting interesting people — including famous actors and some of the great amateur and professional tennis players of the day, men like Bobby Riggs, Pancho Gonzalez, Jack Kramer, the great Donald Budge and Francisco 'Pancho' Segura. As yet, the idea of 'Open' tennis, with pros welcome to compete with the amateurs at Grand Slam tournaments, is just a dream in the minds of the outcast pros.

Gloria is at the Pan-American Tennis Tournament in Mexico City along with her friend and mentor, Wimbledon champion Pauline Betz. Tennis players at the time are a footloose, fun-loving, devil-may-care bunch, none less interested in what the devil may – or may not – give a hang about than Segura, known to all as 'Segu'.

The firstborn of the seven offspring of Domingo Segura Paredes and Francisca Cano, Segura was born prematurely in Ecuador in a bus traveling from Quevedo to Guayaquil. He barely survived. Technically, he was a *cholo*, a child born of a union between a person of superior Spanish blood (Domingo's) and an Indian. The family was poor. A childhood case of rickets left Pancho with permanently and dramatically bowed legs that would one day be famous. He would never grow taller than 5ft 6in.

Domingo worked as a guardian on the estate of a prominent Ecuadorian banker, Don Juan José Medina. The banker became *padrino*, or 'godfather,' to little Pancho. Medina felt that the frail Panchito needed physical activity that would strengthen his muscles, and decided the exercise would be tennis. Medina was a tennis enthusiast, and a member of the board that ran the prestigious Guayaquil Tennis Club. He arranged for Domingo to become head caretaker at the club, an arrangement not unlike the one enjoyed by Arthur Ashe at Brook Field in Richmond, Virginia, two decades later.

Panchito was too frail to compete on the athletic fields of Guayaquil with the other children in his class, but he was fascinated by tennis. Domingo encouraged this healthy obsession; after the *senores* who comprised the club membership left for the evening, Domingo would take Panchito out on one of the club's four hard courts and hit balls with him. While weak, the youngster had boundless energy and the instinctive, natural footwork that has been the hallmark of numerous champions spanning every era.

The youngster also developed a unique style in a sport dominated by coaching and teaching philosophies predicated on the fact that while there are an infinite number of 'wrong' ways to hit a shot, there is also one right way. Panchito could barely lift a tennis racquet (this before 'youth models' are introduced) when he started to play. The honor roll of tennis is littered with champions who started at an age when they had to swing the racquet with both hands, especially on the backhand side. Yet this exception among champions would wind up hitting a one-handed backhand (unlike the man who would be his most successful protégé) and a double-fisted forehand – a shot so unusual that it was often referred to as a 'freak shot'. It wasn't meant in a pejorative way by anyone unfortunate enough to have to deal with it. No less an authority than Jack Kramer, Grand Slam champion and father of the pro tour as we know it, described Segura's forehand as the best shot he'd ever seen, partly because of how well Segu disguised its intended target area, and the acute angles he was able to find thanks to the added leverage of the extra hand.

Panchito was a known and feared player throughout all of Latin American by the time he was seventeen – so much so that he caught the eye of the head coach at the University of Miami, Gardnar Mulloy. Segura would justify Mulloy's gamble by winning the NCAA singles title for three consecutive years, 1943–5 – years during which, among other honors, he was the number three-ranked player in the US and a four-time semi-finalist at the US National Championships.

When he ventured out on to the tournament trail after college, Segu became an instant star. He was exotic looking in a sport overpopulated with impressive specimens of white Anglo-Saxon Protestant conformity. His skin is the color of a chestnut, and his nose erupts from his face like the business end of a hatchet – undoubtedly the legacy of his Inca ancestors.

Moreover, he was famous for the declamations and cries with which he greeted difficult moments during a match, a habit that flaunted the game's reverential attitude toward silence and self-restraint. Even the most stiff-necked Presbyterian couldn't help but chuckle when, with a break-point opportunity, the bow-legged little man from somewhere south exhorted himself to 'Do it, do it now, Pancho!'

Segu also was charismatic and relaxed, always ready with a quip or a dirty joke that would make the heat rise to the faces of the ladies who aren't supposed to like men like Pancho but do anyway. In his generally squeaky clean milieu, Pancho became the rake. The bad boy. The one you wouldn't dare bring home for dinner if you're a certain kind of girl, but with whom you would happily roll around in the back seat of a convertible from sundown until daybreak.

There is a fair amount of that kind of hanky-panky in tennis in this post-war period. The players are more competent at, not to mention more interested in, making love than money — and why not? They inhabit their own island in a sea of sports, one with a self-sustaining environment and unique properties. Some of the players have known each other for a decade or longer. They travel in loose packs and live together under similar circumstances, much like a traveling theater troupe. The women wear short skirts and the men work in short pants; they cavort together under the sun, while their more conventional counterparts wear ties, labor in offices, or play the role of dutiful stay-at-home wives.

In Mexico City, Pancho has his eye on this Gloria Thompson. They are in a hotel room together with a few other players and refreshments, a common enough occurrence at tournaments. She's very pretty in a pulled together, classic way, an apt symbol of the world through which he is cutting a huge swath. She would make a nice trophy, and Pancho senses that his juju is working, for Gloria appears fascinated by his stories and captive to his mischievous sense of humor. He is, after all, one of the very best tennis players in the world. She is one of the many athletic tennis ladies who give the circuit a shot but are destined, for any number of reasons, to partake but briefly of the colorful and glamorous life.

It's all working for Pancho – or so he thinks – until the party is interrupted by noise coming from the next room. The room belongs to actor Gilbert Roland, who has chosen this moment to engage in passionate congress with a young lady friend. Gloria, good Catholic girl that she is, is rattled. She snaps out of the spell Pancho has been weaving and, realizing what she might be letting herself in for, she begins to extricate herself from the situation. Pancho can sense her slipping away but he doesn't really mind. The world is full of pretty girls, not all of them as uptight and easily spooked as this one.

Almost two decades later, Gloria Thompson (now Connors) and Pancho Segura have a reunion of sorts in 1967 in St Louis, where Pancho is playing a one-off pro even though he is officially retired and now the head pro at the Beverly Hills Tennis Club. Gloria brings along Two-Mom and Jimmy, for she has an ulterior motive in this reunion.

Gloria wants Pancho to have a look at her son, Jimmy, or Jimbo. She believes he has world-class talent, and she is wise enough to see that she has taken him as far as she can, teaching him a compact 'woman's' game with which, thanks to his agility and speed, he could bring men to heel. But she is just one of the many supplicants who approach Pancho with more or less the same agenda. They know him by reputation as a superb tactician and motivator; they hope he will accept their children and make champions of them – often regardless of the cost.

Pancho rolls his eyes when Gloria makes her pitch. 'Yeah, yeah. I hear that all the time,' Segura tells her, right to her face. But he and Gloria go back a ways; he feels he owes it to her to at least give the thin, long-limbed boy a look. He suggests that Gloria bring her Jimbo out to California for what essentially would be a tryout for both parties.

Unbeknownst to Gloria or Jimbo, the timing could not have been more perfect. In the months before the Connors book their trip to Los Angeles, his game takes another great jump. And he's that much more comfortable with the curious steel racquet that he's adopted as his weapon of choice. Jimmy watches, amused, as others try out the racquet that does such lethal work in his hands. None of them gives the object anything like the chance it deserves, Jimmy knows; they all – even some of the famous pros, including Billie Jean King and Clark Graebner – give up trying to tame and control it.

Jimbo is different. He's cracked the code. He will tell me, years later, that he more or less 'aims' his shot roughly two and a half or three feet inside the opposite baseline. The more precisely he meets the ball with exactly the right area of the racquet (the notorious 'sweet spot' on the strings, usually a bit closer to the top of the frame than dead center), the closer his shot comes to hitting the lines. The racquet is especially useful for the stroke that becomes Connors' signature shot and his single greatest attribute, the return of serve. The combination of that explosive steel racquet and Connors' athleticism and superb eyesight and reflexes will terrorize his rivals.

The summer of 1968 is waning and Jimbo is approaching his sixteenth birthday when he and Gloria deplane in Los Angeles and take a taxi to the Del Capri hotel. Two-Mom and Pop Thompson, meanwhile, are en route to Los Angeles in Jimbo's own convertible maroon Corvette, which he had purchased a few months earlier for $2,600 with money he had saved doing odd jobs, including some toll-booth work with his dad. Two-Mom and Pop had fantasized aloud about the entrance they would soon make into the City of Angels, where they would also soon find out that nobody, except perhaps their adoring grandson and daughter, really cared.

In fact, there's some question about whether those parties would even still be in Los Angeles when Two-Mom and Pop roll in. Jimbo is on the ground in LA for less than a day when he tells Gloria that he misses his dog. He also misses his brother Johnny. He doesn't really want to make this move – all this before he has even met and worked out for Segura. Gloria takes a map out of her purse, carefully unfolds it and ticks off some landmarks, including the Los Angeles Tennis Club and the Beverly Hills Tennis Club. She suggests that Pop and Jimmy take the Corvette and disappear for the day – just take in the sights, get a feel for the town.

The ploy works beautifully. By nightfall, after Pop and Jimbo had put many miles on the odometer of the 'Vette, Jimmy is besotted with visions of swimming pools, Lamborghinis, palm trees – and tennis courts. Plenty of tennis courts, and beautiful people using them. Jimbo saw the mythic Hollywood sign and some of the homes up in the hills. Back in Belleville, Jimbo's increasing prowess at tennis – he was, by then, among the top five juniors in the country – elicited no more than, at best, a curious shrug. But here – here in Los Angeles, tennis seemed to matter. Jimbo can see that. Here, nobody is going to make fun of him for running around in short white pants.

Gloria has successfully imbued Jimbo with a measure of class resentment, and the conviction that they are 'outsiders'. He's accepted the warning that he must kick and claw and scratch for everything he wants – all the things those 'thems' would not otherwise surrender to him. Yet he is instantly seduced by his exposure to the symbols of the elites of Los Angeles. He tells Gloria that night that there is 'no way' he's going back to Illinois, even though by then the Connors have moved from East St Louis into the more upscale suburb of Belleville.

In the 1960s, Southern California became the most fertile training and proving ground in the history of high-level tennis. The champions who will spring from that soil, or pass through and have their game finished and polished there, include Pancho Gonzalez, Arthur Ashe, Jimmy Connors, Stan Smith, Bob Lutz, Erik van Dillen, Dennis Ralston – and many, many others who would distinguish themselves on the courts of the world. And if this wheel could be said to have a hub, it is Pancho Segura.

By 1961, Segu was separated from his wife, Virginia Spencer Smith, a pretty girl from solid Yankee stock whom he had first met when she was just thirteen years old. At the time her family belonged to the West Side Tennis Club, where the US Nationals were played, but her parents later divorced and Virginia wound up living in an apartment with her mother in the enclave of Forest Hills, where the WSTC is located. Pancho and Virginia eloped when he was twenty-six and she just nineteen;

the New York tabloids had a field day. The couple had one child, Spencer Francisco Segura, who was born in July 1952. His father was away playing tennis at the time.

The itinerant pro's way of life accelerated the ruination of Segu's first marriage. By '61, he is newly married to a woman with three children from a previous marriage, California blueblood Beverley Moylan Young. Less than a year later, Segura gives up his life as a touring professional to accept a position as the head coach at the Beverly Hills Tennis Club. The club was founded in 1929, in response to the Los Angeles Tennis Club's prohibition against accepting members who are in the film industry, or Jews – policies no longer in place today. Over the decades, the BHTC prospered and became a magnet for Hollywood elites, including such luminaries as Dina Shore, Charlton Heston, Lauren Bacall, Robert Evans, Gene Hackman, Ava Gardner and Julie Andrews.

The circumstances at the club are pleasant enough: Pancho earns between $15 and $25 per hour teaching those who are often fundamentally unteachable due to a lack of serious interest, talent or both. He bats around balls with famous Hollywood producers and actors, encourages starlets with saucy double entendres that leave them thinking this tennis stuff could be more fun than it first appears. He patiently works with the children of those same members, even when those kids are just going through the motions in order to please their A-type parents.

The social life that comes along with all of this is appealing to Segu, not least because of the entrée his second wife provides to society in Los Angeles. But Segu is also a man who never, ever loses his passion and relish for the game of tennis played at its very highest level, the peaks at which he and his likes, including Jack Kramer, Bobby Riggs, Pancho Gonzalez, have competed.

Thus, Segura becomes a guru in tennis-drenched Los Angeles. When he is not otherwise engaged at the club, he is up in Pasadena, helping a local tennis philanthropist run the program that will produce Stan Smith. Players cognizant of his reputation as a master tactician will make pilgrimages to the Beverly Hills Tennis Club, where the board is wise enough to relax member-guest rules to allow Segura to work with whom he wants, when and where he wants. Segu's son Spencer will remember days when the weakest players engaged on any of the club's four courts are a couple of Australians named John Newcombe and Tony Roche.

This also is why Jimmy Connors is as great a find for Segu as the veteran coach is for the weedy youngster whose drive and desire are so striking. Whatever Segu is meant to be, it isn't the guy who feeds balls to the wife of the most successful dentist in a twenty-mile radius.

Segura looks for two out of three qualities in a player whom he will deign to recognize as a legitimate prospect: excellent movement/footwork, an outstanding serve, or a dangerous serve return. Jimbo meets the criteria, lacking only the fearsome serve. But he has an additional attribute that really convinces Segura that Jimbo has enormous potential – a backhand that he hits relatively flat, but with an enormous amount of upper-body rotation. The result is a laser-like ball that whistles low over the net and, time and again, leaves an opponent lunging and scrambling, hopelessly out of position. At the time, the two-handed backhand is a relative rarity, but Segura knows full well the value of hitting with both hands on the handle.

But there is more. Segura also sees something of himself in Jimbo – a vestige of that outsider bent on conquering a world not his own. Jimbo has a quality that can't be taught and has nothing to do with what commonly passes for talent. 'Jimmy,' he tells him. 'I love your pride. I can see you have big balls.'

Almost as an afterthought, Segura adds, 'And – you are coachable.'

This final quality of Jimbo's, while an enormous asset, will also become the source of mounting friction between Gloria and Segura. For Gloria's great strength, her love for her son, is also the source of her greatest weakness – the inability to let go, to trust others with Jimbo. Her paranoid instincts are already flickering when she warns Segura not to tamper with Jimmy's game, meaning the mechanics of how he hits the ball, and his fast-paced baseline style which is built on a foundation of excellent groundstrokes. It's the other, tactical and strategic elements of the game that she wants the coach to focus on.

Segura listens politely and assures the obsessive stage mother that all would be as she asks. Then he goes about making the single most significant change that enables Jimmy to transcend and improve upon his solid education in the fundamentals. Aware of his protégé's quickness and the relatively flat trajectory of his ground-strokes (particularly that spectacular backhand), Segura has Jimbo move up to the baseline from his familiar rallying zone two feet behind it and tells him to play from as close to the line, or as far inside it, as he is able.

This may seem like a familiar tactical theme by now, but at the time it wasn't. And it is exactly the kind of insight on which Segura has built his reputation. He knows that Jimbo can 'run like a deer', and that ability combined with his solid groundstrokes adds up to a load of wins in the junior ranks. But even with Jimbo's athleticism, prancing around the court hitting nice strokes can only take you so far. Segura knows this, which is why the last thing he really cares about is nice strokes.

In moving Jimbo up, Segura is unleashing the whirlwind. For, by taking the ball on the rise from just inside the court, Jimbo can ratchet up the pace, take time away from his opponent, harass, harry and run him into the ground. It's the equivalent of removing the governor from an internal combustion engine; the vehicle can now move much faster, even as the danger that it may spin out and crash increases dramatically. Segura isn't worried about that. Not with this ferret-faced youngster with the cheesy Prince Valiant haircut and eyes that gleam like tiny black lacquered buttons as he decimates one practice partner after another.

Once Segura has put Jimbo in touch with his aggressive instincts, he begins a long process of teaching him how to play intelligent, situational tennis. You take chances with your shots and tactics when you are comfortably ahead — or desperately behind. In that vast middle territory that accounts for most of a match, or even the meat of a single game, you play the percentages. In order to neutralize or attack an opponent's weakness, sometimes you must go through his strength. When you see a second serve, you attack it.

None of this is rocket science. The wisdom of the tennis ages is imparted to Jimbo in small doses, sometimes jotted on cocktail napkins as he sits huddled with Segura over breakfast. The boy is like a sponge, and much later Segura would say: 'I worked with Jimbo because I believed in him. Everyone who saw him play said he was too small and that he didn't have enough of a serve. But they didn't see that Jimbo was a killer. In his head, he had everything. It didn't matter how big you were. He wasn't afraid. He could destroy you.'

With a hyper-aggressive sensibility, that gleaming steel racquet and a chip the size of a manhole cover on his shoulder, Jimbo is poised to do great damage to the establishment he's been trained to resent even as he covets — and partakes of — its remunerations.

Spencer Segura wants nothing more than the affection and attention of his father, the father who was not present at his birth; the father who left Spencer in the clutches of a stepfather who, among other things, makes the boy get rid of the dog he loves; the father who seems to have time for everyone but Spencer, and who lives a robust, glamorous social life that, regrettably, doesn't really include his son.

By the age of sixteen, Spencer could easily be the sympathetic victim in a sobering, cautionary tale. He could be a drug addict, or a hit-and-run driver, his failings a testament to the psychological impact of a family break-up, parental neglect and the perils of having a celebrity parent. But Spencer is no such thing. He is just an extremely likeable and smart boy who already shows signs of being as much of a realist as his famously shrewd and ruthless father. Spencer has figured out that the only way to get time with his real father, to be around him at all, is to spend a lot of time at the Beverly Hills Tennis Club.

When the Connors clan shows up at the BHTC and, in the blink of an eye, declares for Los Angeles, Pancho turns to Spencer and says, 'Go get Jimmy into school.'

'What school?' Spencer asks. 'When?'

'Your school. He's going with you.'

Spencer makes a few phone calls and in no time at all Jimmy is enrolled at Rexford High School. It's very different from Assumption High in East St Louis, where getting a homeless bum to buy you a pint of flavored wine was about the epitome of teenage mischief. The youthful hormones at Rexford are in some cases fueled by sex and drugs and rock and roll. Jimmy doesn't even know what some of his classmates are taking to get high; he just knows he wants no part of it — a conviction that was powerfully reinforced when a fellow scholar overdosed right in front of Jimmy at 10.15 in the morning in the school parking lot.

When Spencer first takes Jimmy around to meet his Beverly Hills friends, some call him 'cornpone'. Spencer runs with a precocious brat pack consisting of, among others, Dino Martin (son of Dean), Desi Arnaz (son of Desi Arnaz Jr) and Billy Hinsche — youngsters who formed the teeny-bopper band Dino, Desi, and Billy. Long before Jimmy suddenly arrives on the scene, Dino's mother Jeanne has taken a genuine, sweet interest in Spencer. She sees how well-meaning Spencer is and perhaps thinks that he is attention-starved and confused — the son of a man she perceives to be a celebrity-hungry tennis coach. The boy only picked up the game, despite a talent that would soon be manifest, after his father took the job that stationed him at the Beverly Hills

Tennis Club. Spencer was happy to go to the club every day, less from any innate desire to play tennis than to get the chance to be around his father.

Still, given Pancho's habits and the discomfort Spencer feels around his stepfather, the boy becomes something of a *Flying Dutchman*. He spends many nights sleeping at the home of the Martins. Other times, Norman Kreiss, another Hollywood elite whose three sons all play high-level tennis, gathers Spencer up with his own kids and takes them all home for dinner and a sleepover.

Spencer is Jimbo's great advocate; he is, after all, the most secure line tying Spencer to his father. Spencer repeats Pancho's prophecy about Jimbo's destiny, and the budding player is accepted into Spencer's social set. Pancho also takes it upon himself to help ease Jimbo's transition to the laid-back California way of life. The boys are allowed to have a drink before or with dinner and Pancho, who knows as much about women as he does about tennis, makes sure the boys don't end up confused and awkward adolescents, wasting precious time as they ponder the mysteries associated with a remote, fairer sex.

The kids in this voluptuary group have a remarkable degree of freedom and some will pay an undeclared price – their innocence, their capacity to wonder at an unfolding world. Their role models in these, the most potent years of the 'Swinging Sixties', are adults who gaily banter about the infidelities regularly occurring in their set. At the Beverly Hills Tennis Club they don't like to call dalliances anything as lurid as 'cheating', or anything as grave as indulging in an 'affair'. They like to describe it as 'nesting', as if the participants were two precious and lovingly domestic bluebirds.

But Spencer and Jimmy avoid the worst of the temptations. They assiduously steer clear of most reckless behaviors. As much as Spencer helps make Jimmy's life easier, the newcomer also makes a serious contribution to his sponsor. His single-minded focus on tennis inspires and challenges Spencer. If he is to continue building his relationship with his father, he must keep up with Jimmy.

Their life, for different reasons, is built around the BHTC. To an outsider, it still appears a dissolute life. Days are spent either on the court or sitting around by the pool, ogling the pretty young things and playing backgammon (Jimmy is finished with school for the day by the time Rexford High has it's 10.15 a.m. nutrition break; then it's off to the club). At night, the boys are left to their own devices.

Occasionally, the boys drop by the Daisy Club, an ultra-exclusive private club and discotheque on Rodeo Drive. It was created for the most well-connected of Hollywood personages, including the likes of Frank Sinatra and Warren Beatty; the total membership barely numbers over one hundred yet it includes Pancho

Segura. One evening, the boys show up at the unmarked door of the club. They ring, and the slot in the door at eye-level slides back. A moment later, the door swings back and Jane Fonda, bored and happy to play doorman, steps back to welcome them inside.

The bartender at the Daisy Club feels no moral culpability for serving his trademark whiskey sours to the boys. One evening at the club, Frank Sinatra strolls over to where the boys are having dinner with an acquaintance from high school. He asks if the boys want to see a show, then takes them to a recording studio where Spencer and Jimmy are the only outsiders watching as Sinatra records three songs.

But for all the freedom the boys enjoy, Segura is no indifferent or otherwise occupied parent whose parental philosophy is 'out of sight, out of mind'. Apart from any parental responsibility he feels, he has an obvious, personal stake in Jimmy Connors' future, as well as a daily investment in his present. He insists on certain things, the chief among them that tennis − not the game of tennis, but the work of becoming a tennis player − always comes first.

Thus, the boys have a 10 p.m. curfew. When they get haircuts, skin must show above the ears or they are sent back to the barber. Liquor or women? 'Girls are okay,' Pancho tells the youngsters. 'In fact, if you want them I will help get them for you.' Liquor in moderation is no big thing, either. But cigarettes? Heaven help anyone whom Segura catches with a whiff of stale cigarette smoke on his clothes.

When Gloria, Two-Mom, Pop and Jimbo first arrive in Los Angeles, they rent a third-floor walk-up apartment. But the punishing climb is too much for Two-Mom, who is a smoker. The Connors eventually bite the bullet and rent a two-bedroom ground-floor apartment on Wilshire Boulevard, although they have to come up with $400 a month in rent, much higher than they had hoped to pay.

Once the women feel that Jimmy is well established and Segura understands what Gloria does – and doesn't – want, the clan returns to Belleville. When Gloria is in Los Angeles, she does a little bit of tennis coaching and also waits tables at a joint on Wilshire, Nibblers Restaurant, a place that is still open today and has been described by critics as 'a classic – in that tacky carpet, orange upholstery, "senior special" kind of way'.

Each month, Pop diligently sends twenty bucks from his social security check to help cover expenses. A constant exposure to tight budgets, and the unease and simmering resentment Jimbo feels at having to see Gloria in a waitress's uniform, tapping her pencil against the pad while a fickle customer tries to decide between the meatloaf and a fried fish platter, only increases his determination to let no distraction interfere with his tennis training. He could never betray Gloria by slacking off, or putting anything before tennis. He will master the game, and use it to cash in, to make enough money for Gloria never to have to swing a racquet, or the double doors leading into the kitchen, again.

It turns out to be a promise not too difficult to keep. He has great trouble concentrating on schoolwork, perhaps because on a typical day he's there barely long enough to know the biology lab from the lavatory. Yet he's not merely able but actually eager to spend five hours a day on the tennis court. Some aspects of the code by which tennis players of Segura's vintage lived rub off on Connors, despite the contempt he feels for the 'thems' who populate the tennis world, with their phony etiquette and effeminate good manners. He will always remember Segura telling him: 'All I ask is that you believe in yourself. No negative thoughts, no excuses. Lose like a man and win like a man. If you're injured, don't play. If you play, you're not injured. Always give 100 per cent and I'll be happy.'

The Hollywood swells make it easier for Connors to get a jump on his aspirations to wealth without having to bag groceries or mow lawns. All the stars want to hit with the best young tennis players available, and soon Spencer and Jimbo are playing doubles for $20 per set – starting at a 0-4 disadvantage. Eventually, the friends become just too good and they are obliged to split up to make things interesting. Jimmy usually takes on the weaker player from the other team as a partner.

Film producer Bob Evans (responsible for such classics as *Love Story* and *The Godfather*) would later claim that he played over forty matches with Jimmy Connors as a partner without ever having won a single set – a detail that the good-natured Evans put down to his theory that Connors and Segura were actively colluding to do what was best for their little business.

All this time, the games of both boys are developing at an accelerated rate. Segura runs them mercilessly, laughing when a drill ends and they both collapse in an exhausted heap before Segura stops chortling and tells them, with a straight face, that this is exactly what they should expect when they finally meet the real competition.

Segura's deep bag of tricks contains one additional element that is easy to dismiss as hooey, but is critically valuable. He tells Jimbo, over and over, time and again, day after day, that he is 'the greatest'. Segura knows that when you tell that to a certain kind of person, he will be inclined to believe you. Jimmy is that kind of person to start with, but there's another reason to build him up so transparently. The shortest among the top player in Connors age group are six-footers Brian Gottfried and Erik van Dillen.

Connors, at best the no. 4 junior in the US during his first year with Segura, is a scrawny 5ft 10in, and he has that strange two-handed backhand. He is such an unprepossessing figure that on one occasion van Dillen, the most highly touted of the juniors in his age division, refuses even to play a match with him on the grounds that Connors is 'too small'.

The renown of Segura and the feverish tennis activity in the Los Angeles area ensures that Jimmy gets plenty of competition. Everyone he plays has a different, explosive weapon. Spencer and Stan Smith have monstrous serves; nobody volleys like van Dillen; Gottfried's slice backhand is superb. The game is a moveable feast; one day Spencer and Jimmy are playing up at UCLA, the next they are at the Los Angeles Tennis Club, then over at the Kreiss's private court. At the BHTC, you never knew when one of Segura's old buddies – Bobby Riggs, Ken Rosewall, Roy Emerson – would drop by, and you never knew if he needed a hitting partner.

Jimbo's game grows exponentially while he is under Segura's tutelage, so much so that at one stage Pancho brags to Jack Kramer and Bobby Riggs that Jimbo can beat the top American junior, van Dillen. His two interlocutors scoff and ask if he is kidding. Pancho tells them he's not, and that he's willing to bet money – not just a little money, but $10,000 – that Jimbo can take Erik. Segura's astonished friends say they'll take that bet. They go off to raise the money and spread word among their well-heeled connections, and soon a parade of bettors and backers is lined up by both sides and the original bet increases to $50,000 and then to $100,000.

But Jimbo has no time to waste; he's getting better and better, and his destiny is obvious to anyone with a pair of eyes. He will be great, perhaps the greatest. Before the details of the match with van Dillen can be arranged and finalized, the high-rollers who had been ready to back van Dillen all think better of their decision and pull their bets.

CHAPTER FIVE

The Professionals

'There are two people in my life I would trust with my life: my father and Donald Dell.'

Arthur Ashe

'Playing tennis was my thing, but I eventually got a Ph.D. in marketing and promotion from [Bill] Riordan University.'

Jimmy Connors

Stan Smith is a twenty-one-year-old protégé of Pancho Segura. He met Arthur Ashe when both of them were part of a loosely organized group playing under the supervision of Segura thanks to the underwriters of the program, the Pasadena Tennis Patrons. Smith was an eager student, while Ashe and the likes of Charlie Pasarell, Dennis Ralston and many others (including, at one point, Billie Jean King) were both hitting partners and mentors. Smith went on to the University of Southern California, whose Trojans were the hated rivals of Ashe's UCLA Bruins.

In the summer of 1968, after Smith sweeps the NCAA singles and doubles (with Bob Lutz) championships, he leaves behind the heady collegiate days of cheerleaders, pom-poms and rah-rah rivalries. He and Ashe are team-mates on the US Davis Cup squad, and playing not just for themselves, or even their respective colleges. They are playing for the nation, and it is a republic cruelly stung by an unexpected loss to Ecuador the previous year. It was a loss some would call the worst in US Davis Cup history. It was a loss that, years later, Ashe himself would call 'the lowest point in my career, the absolute nadir'. He had good reason to feel that way; Ashe was beaten twice in the singles by relatively unknown journeymen, Miguel Olvera and Pancho Guzman.

United States captain George MacCall was unceremoniously dumped after that loss; it was almost five years since the US, the most successful nation in Davis Cup history, had failed to secure the trophy. McCall's replacement was an ambitious twenty-nine-year-old lawyer and former top junior, Donald Dell – the same Dell who in Charlottesville sixteen years earlier had dashed the hopes of Dr Robert Walter Johnson's first promising African American protégé, Willie Winn.

Smith is a junior champion and a tall (6ft 4in), blond-haired, blue-eyed native of Pasadena, a city most famous for its annual Parade of Roses. This odd cultural ritual is a convincing emblem of the manifest luxuries and joys of life in Southern California. But Smith doesn't see the world through rose-colored glasses, nor harbor the sense of entitlement sometimes found in gifted young athletes. He is a socially conscious young man, and both he and Ashe are already substantially more than mere players under the command of the fiercely liberal coach, Dell.

This is why, in the early days of June 1968, Smith and Ashe are traveling up and down the coast of California, campaigning for Democratic Party presidential candidate Robert F. Kennedy. Dell, in addition to being Davis Cup captain at twenty-eight bucks a day, is a political operative for the Kennedys — has been since he fell under the spell of Camelot as a frequent guest of the tennis-loving Kennedys, and a fixture in their summer entertainments, at the Kennedy family compound in Hyannis Port, Ma.

In 1968 Dell is entrusted with supervising the advance men for the Democratic primary election effort in five states, including California. Smith and Ashe do their campaigning the old-fashioned way, on the back end of a caboose that is hauled by rail from one whistle stop to another during the last hectic days of the campaign — Sunday and Monday, 3 and 4 June. As soon as they finish at the last stop, Dell and his players fly to Charlotte to prepare to avenge the US's loss the previous year to Ecuador on slow red clay in Guayaquil — this time, on a fast indoor surface suited to the games of Ashe and the other first-choice singles player Clark Graebner.

The news that Robert F. Kennedy has been shot three times as he makes his way through the kitchen of a Los Angeles hotel in order to avoid the press and his deliriously happy supporters breaks shortly after mid-night of 5 June. On the 7th, Ashe demolishes Guzman, Graebner crushes Olvera and the US goes on to sweep Ecuador 5-0, while losing a grand total of just one set – that in the fourth match, a 'dead rubber'.

But a somber mood hangs over the American squad, and even this commanding performance seems less meaningful than it might have under different circumstances.

Donald Dell first meets Arthur Ashe in 1965, at a tournament in Fort Worth, Texas. He's eager to see the twenty-two-year-old player, and he can still remember that Willie Winn kid who was developed by the same African American coach who would teach Ashe. Dell remembers how puzzled he was by Winn's charitable nature, as expressed in the generous calls Winn made on behalf of Dell whenever a ball fell anywhere near a line – as per Dr Johnson's first commandment for survival in the white-dominated sport.

Dell is fresh out of law school, and while he's twenty-six years old he has kept his hand in in the game. He's taking another crack at the tour that has not treated him too kindly. He eventually meets Ashe in that Fort Worth tournament and will not forget the whippet lean African-American who serves him off the court with such authority that it contributes to Dell's growing realization that perhaps the law isn't such a boring profession after all. Within a year, Dell is hard at work at the Washington law firm Hogan and Hartson.

Dell penetrates the inner circle of the Kennedys thanks to Sargent Shriver, who was married to Eunice Kennedy, sister of the three most prominent Kennedys of the 1960s, John, Robert and Edward. Dell's first job is that of 'special assistant' to Shriver; it's a formidable, vaguely mysterious job description that Dell — a man who has always liked to cut to the chase — will years later describe more accurately as being 'the guy who carries the briefcase. It was a helluva briefcase.'

Despite his rapid rise in Democratic political circles, Dell is still a tennis player. The tragedy that shook his world in 1968 is accompanied by an equally stunning and happier event in the parallel universe of tennis — the lords of tennis finally agree to open the major tournaments, including the four Grand Slams, to professional as well as amateur players. Up until this momentous decision is taken, only amateurs were allowed to compete in the sanctioned tournaments administered by the International Lawn Tennis Federation (ILTF; later, the 'Lawn' would be abandoned) and its national affiliates, including Britain's Lawn Tennis Association (LTA) or the US's United States Lawn Tennis Association (today, the USTA). As a private club, Wimbledon is not controlled by the LTA or the ITF, but it does work hand-in-hand with those organizations.

The key point is that once amateurs established themselves as marketable tennis stars by winning major tournaments, they wanted to cash in on financial opportunities, not play for expense money, pretty trophies or even the under-the-table appearance fees that were common in some places at the time. But because they elected to play for money, they were barred from the most important tournaments in the world. Shut out, they mounted barnstorming tours of their own. Often they traveled from city to city, a rolled-up court stashed in the back of a station wagon.

This was a system in which everyone lost. The prestige of a tournament like Wimbledon was diminished because the best, proven players turned pro and were banned. The great players suffered because they were unable to compete at the best-known venues against all the best players. The amateurs suffered because they had no chance to test themselves against the great pros, all of whom had once been amateurs themselves. The advent of the Open era, in which the artificial barriers were dropped and all players were entitled to play all tournaments for which they qualified, sounded the death knell for players who saw some advantage in

right: Young Arthur Ashe beaming as he shows off his earliest collection of trophies – a trove destined to increase exponentially as he becomes a Grand Slam champion who played in seven major finals (winning three). © Arthur Ashe Learning Center

below: Ashe (far right) and doubles partner Hubert Easton exchange a collegial, post-match handshake with their opponents after a match on the lawns of Forest Hills (home of the U.S. National Championships and later the U.S. Open) in 1959. *Harry Harris/Press Association Images*

left: Gloria and Jimmy Connors, waiting for a Wimbledon courtesy car at the entrance to London's Westbury Ho[tel]
© *Press Association Images*

below: A rare photograp[h] of Jimmy Connors with his parents. 'Big Jim' Connors and his wife Gloria were estranged, with Jim playing almost no role in his son's life once Gloria and the young Jimmy moved to Los Angeles.
© *John D. Hanlon /Sports Illustrated/Getty Images*

bove: Ashe introduces his father to the crowd during the trophy presentation
:eremony following his first US Open win. © *Hulton Archive/Getty Images*

above: An informal strategy session for Connors (left) with the two Panchos who heavily influenced his career, Segura (center) and Gonzalez.
© *Eric Schweikardt/Sports Illustrated/Getty Images*

below: Connors, playfully sitting astride his friend and frequent doubles partner, Ilie Nastase. The two were the most entertaining – and controversial – stars wherever they joined forces. Their antics didn't always sit well with their opponents who frequently felt relegated to supporting cast by the pair. © *Michael Cole*

right: Connors performing the familiar leap over the net after another win. The flamboyant gesture was about the only 'traditional' aspect of those Las Vegas exhibition extravaganzas. © *Todd Friedman*

below: 'Team Connors' (from left to right: Bill Riordan, Pancho Segura, Jimmy and Gloria Connors) are all smiles in advance of the much ballyhooed 'heavyweight challenge match' pitting Connors against the aging Australian star and tennis icon, Rod Laver. © *Tony Triolo/ Sports Illustrated/ Getty Images*

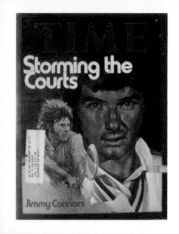

left: The swath Connors cut through tennis in 1974 combined with his showmanship earned him a cover story in *Time* magazine – at the time, the leading news magazine in the United States and elsewhere. © *Art Seitz*

left: The men's Wimbledon champion of 1974 receives a heartfelt kiss from the female champion that year, Chris Evert. Journalists dubbed it the 'love double' but the high-profile romance was destined to end in broken engagement less than a full year later.
© *Keystone-France/ Gamma-Keystone via Getty Images*

right: Ashe, turning to the player guest box at Wimbledon at the moment of victory. The reaction was so spontaneous that Ashe was whirling and thrusting his fist in the air before the scoreboard had even changed to record the end of the 1975 Wimbledon final.

© *Ed Lacey/ Popperfoto/ Getty Images*

left: Ashe, still wearing his Team USA Davis Cup jacket, beams as he holds aloft the greatest prize in men's tennis, the cup awarded the Wimbledon singles champion. As sports trophies go, it is one of the smaller ones, measuring barely 18-inches in height.

© *Tony Triolo/Sports Illustrated/Getty Images*

left: Ashe, holding his official notice of induction into the International Tennis Hall of Fame in Newport, Rhode Island. Not much later the new, main stadium at the U.S. Open would be named after him as well.

© *Los Angeles Times/Press Association Images*

right: Connors captured the attention of the sporting world and thrilled the crowds at the U.S. Open in 1991, when he made an astonishing run to the semifinals at the age of thirty-nine. He retired with a record unlikely to ever be challenged: 109 tournament victories.

© *Caryn Levy/Sports Illustrated/Getty Images*

retaining their amateur status, or simply weren't good enough to become professionals.

Tennis rapidly entered a new era in 1968, one that would soon give rise to the concept of cradle-to-grave professionalism. One interesting holdout against professionalism was (and remains) the US collegiate establishment. College stars in all sports in the US forfeit their scholarships and/or right to compete if they play for pay. Apart from that, by the 1960s all the popular sports had long embraced professionalism — even tennis's sister sport, golf.

At the time of this momentous transition, Ashe is fast approaching twenty-five — by which time he's played in the US Nationals, soon to be rechristened the US Open, for nine years. He's developed steadily and risen incrementally. After leading UCLA to the national collegiate championship with wins in the singles and doubles in 1965, he struck his first great blow as an international player with a sensational win at Forest Hills in the US Nationals over defending champion (as well as recent Wimbledon champion) Roy Emerson.

The wins at the international level of Davis Cup and Grand Slam play begin to pile up. Ashe travels with the US Davis Cup team, and he plays all the major tournaments. He makes back-to-back Australian Open finals in 1965 and 1966, where Emerson extracts double payback for Ashe's career-launching 1965 triumph over him at Forest Hills.

Yet even in his early twenties, Ashe's prospect of earning a living from prize money and endorsements is remote. Thus, he feels no great urgency to turn pro, nor is he concerned that some driven youngster will eclipse him and lower his market value. As a Davis Cup player, he enjoys enormous prestige. While his younger brother Johnnie will serve in Marine Corps during the Vietnam War, Arthur Jr, along with Stan Smith, Bob Lutz, Donald Dell and others, tour US military outposts in Southeast Asia (and other tennis hotbeds, like Alaska). These are goodwill tours, although some might find them uncomfortably close to propaganda events.

In any event, the young men have a great time — especially in places like Bangkok and Saigon, where they are encouraged by their high-powered hosts and government officials to partake of all the pleasures on offer, including the available young women. The only one to refuse carnal delights is Stan Smith, who will then be saddled with a nickname that will trail him throughout his distinguished career: 'Mr Clean'.

In some ways, the State Department-sponsored tours are a charade that leave Ashe feeling sobered and almost ashamed of his good fortune. Many of the wounded soldiers the players visit are in bad shape, and most of them have no idea who the tennis players are and, if they know tennis at all, think of it as a toff sport. Because of both his brother's status and his own unique history, Ashe is sensitive to such ironies. But by serving in the US

Army and retaining his amateur status (a condition demanded by the service), he at least avoids the life of a foot soldier.

Since graduating college, Ashe's only responsibilities have been to his career. Free to focus all his efforts on tennis, his game creeps up a few more notches. By early 1968, tennis wheelers and dealers can detect a whiff of the sweeping changes that will soon enable tennis to explode on the sporting landscape. It is Ashe's last year in the army. Things are changing, quickly.

Promoter Dave Dixon – with backing from the keenly observant investor Lamar Hunt – launches a professional tour on the strength of having signed personal services contracts with 'the Handsome Eight' – or, as one wag suggested, 'the Handsome Seven and Tony Roche'. He's interested in recruiting Ashe to his tour. At the same time, tennis insider and entrepreneur George MacCall is running a show called 'the National Tennis League', which is stocked with such bankable pros as Rod Laver, Ken Rosewall, Fred Stolle and others – all refugees from the moribund amateur or 'closed' game. The only thing MacCall lacks is a major American star. He would love to secure Ashe.

Then, in the spring, Wimbledon officials act decisively. Theoretically the most conservative of all tennis stake-holders, they're also the most savvy and self-protective. Their collective ear to the ground, they decide that the only way the game would flourish as anything other than a la-di-da exercise is to allow the professionals to play at the great tournaments. After all, they clearly are the best players in the world; almost every outstanding amateur has gone on to a pro career – robbing the Grand Slam tournaments of big names just as soon as they are made. Besides, the professionals have made serious inroads, credibility-wise. The public has an appetite for tennis and whoever is going to give them the best players will emerge the winner. The die is cast. Wimbledon's Grand Slam counterparts in Australia, France and the US fall into line, partly because they know that if Open tennis is good for Wimbledon it's bound to be good for them.

Starting in April 1968, the game is truly open. Amateurs are still welcome to play, but they must compete with the pros. Predictably, a pro wins the first 'open' Grand Slam event, as the French Open title goes to Ken Rosewall. It's even less surprising when the Wimbledon championship is secured by another iconic Australian, Rod Laver. He had a glorious amateur record at Wimbledon, but then turned professional and spent six years in exile.

It's difficult to say why tennis experienced such enormous growth in the late 1960s and 1970s that the period was officially dubbed 'the tennis boom'. It's easy to postulate that a game played by individuals, filled with interesting characters, was just what the public wanted in what might be called the 'do your own thing' era, or the 'swingin' sixties'. After all, this was the dawn of the era when prestige began to shift from those who were considered part of 'society' to those who could be described as 'celebrities'. Perhaps counter-intuitively, the traditions of the game stood out in stark contrast to the casual and informal mores that led men to abandon their suits and ties in favor of Nehru jackets and bell-bottom jeans that flapped like mainsails in a stiff breeze when the wearer traipsed down Haight Street. The Australians, led by Lew Hoad, Ken Rosewall and Rod Laver, enjoyed enormous success in the late amateur era and, what with their picturesque slang and clean-cut looks, their appeal was less conventional than exotic. Because tennis is a game of individual confrontation between scantily clad men and women, it's easy to pick heroes and villains. Historically, tennis thrives when it features players whose personalities are as colourful or intriguing as their games.

Finally, tennis boomed at a time of great prosperity in the US. Thus, both the native, aspirational nature of tennis and the plain old snob appeal of the game were powerful factors driving its growth. The Open era gave large numbers of people a peek into the rarefied environment of places like Wimbledon, or Forest Hills (where the US National Championships – and US Open – were played for so long). Being egalitarians, Americans felt they could get a piece of the good life through tennis, and they encouraged their children to play the game. They flocked in droves to tennis clubs and paid relatively large sums to play indoors. Commercial genius took care of the rest, fanning the flames of tennis interest. The amount of money paid for the broadcast rights to Wimbledon by the American television network NBC not only poured riches into the coffers of the club, it legitimized the tournament in the eyes of the American public. The process had a salutary effect back in the UK as well because the world was shrinking.

In August 1968, as the game begins to swell in the public mind thanks to Open tennis, MacCall takes Ashe to a Schrafft's automat in New York — a novel cafeteria where the sandwiches and slices of pie all sit in cubby holes behind transparent doors — and offers him $400,000 over five years to join the NTL tour.

Ashe is stunned. It's crazy money to him. He admits he has never even *heard of* that much money. He tells MacCall that he will think about it. While Ashe is mulling over the offer, his Davis Cup captain Donald Dell — a lawyer who believes in the sanctity of the contract — warns him, 'You only sign once.' Dell also tells Ashe that, given the increasing competition among sports promoters, $80,000 per year may not be such a mind-blowing deal after all. Ashe thinks about it. If MacCall is willing to give him that much in August, what might he offer should Ashe win the US Open, or help the US retain the Davis Cup? He decides to tell MacCall that he will make his final decision after the December Davis Cup finals.

At the ensuing US Open, Wimbledon champion and top seed Laver is upset by the lowest seed, no. 16 Cliff Drysdale. It's an enormous break for US Army first lieutenant and US Open no. 5 seed Arthur Ashe Jr (he would lose eighteen consecutive matches to 'Rocket' Rod Laver before he finally cracked the code in 1973). Ashe then handles Drysdale in four sets, after which he lays a similar beating on his Davis Cup team-mate and friend, no. 7 seed Clark Graebner (that semi-final match becomes the basis of John McPhee's delightful book *Levels of the Game*).

Arthur Ashe is in the US Open final. His opponent is Tom Okker, who has earned the rather unimaginative nickname 'the Flying Dutchman' thanks to his speed and quickness. Okker has an all-around, versatile game, anchored in an excellent forehand. His game is marred only by a lack of the one thing Ashe has in abundance: power.

Ashe wins the match in five sets, 14-12, 5-7, 6-3, 3-6, 6-3 – thereby becoming the first man of black African descent to win a major tournament. Because he is in the US Army and obliged to retain his amateur status, Ashe cannot collect the $14,000 winner's purse; the pot goes to Okker, while Ashe receives a grand total of $280 – fourteen days of expenses at $20 a day.

Ashe becomes not only the first African American to win the a major title, he also earns a measure of fame as the first US Open champion, and one even more

noteworthy honor that is unlikely ever to be eclipsed –
Ashe has won a pro Grand Slam tournament as an
amateur. During the trophy presentation ceremony,
Ashe is joined by an elderly black man impeccably
dressed in a dark suit and matching, conservative tie.
Arthur Ashe Sr has just watched his son make history.

In December 1968, Ashe leads the US Davis Cup squad
to a sweep of Australia in the final, Challenge Round.
A few weeks later, he is discharged from the army, and
declares himself a tennis professional. By the late winter
of 1968–9, entrepreneurs and agents of every description
are hot on the trail of Ashe. The most prominent among
them is Mark McCormack, who is laying the founda-
tions for his sports management firm, International
Management Group.

By then, Dell and Ashe have become fast friends. Dell
believes Ashe ought to meet with McCormack, and he
personally trundles him off to three separate interviews
with the man (to some Ashe and Dell loyalists, the
parallels with the biblical Temptations on the Mount
will be as inescapable as they are absurd). Much to Dell's
disdain, McCormack likes to have his breakfast meetings
at Raffles, in the hipster Lexington Hotel in New York, a
place that the all-business, strait-laced lawyer finds a
little too pretentious. After their final interview there,
Ashe and Dell hop into a taxi on Lexington Avenue, and

Ashe turns to Dell and asks, 'How many more times are you going to take me to meet McCormack?'

'Well, I think he's the best,' Dell replies. 'He just signed Jean-Claude Killy, off the Olympics in 1968. He's building something.'

'Why don't you do it?'

'Do what?'

'Manage me, and be my lawyer. If you did it, Stan [Smith] will join us. It will be fun, and we'll have a business.'

'No,' Dell says. 'I'm going back to Hogan and Hartson. I'm going to be the next great trial lawyer.' He can't help adding, 'I'm going to be the next Clarence Darrow.'

Within two weeks, Dell decides that the next Leopold and Loeb will have to wait; Ashe and Smith will come first.

Jimmy Connors knows who Arthur Ashe is. Like everyone else who is anybody in tennis, the new US Open champion used to come to hit at the Beverly Hills Tennis Club at the invitation of Pancho Segura. The other Pancho, Gonzalez, also knows Ashe. All three of them – Segura, Gonzalez and Ashe – are dark-skinned. Pancho collectively refers to them as the 'brown bodies' – but Connors needn't worry about where the sympathies of either Pancho lie. Both men are hard cases. They know all too well about discrimination and racism, but they don't give a shit about the color of your skin, or how much it is — or isn't — like theirs. The only thing that matters to them is how you answer the implicit question, 'Are you a player?'

Jimbo has just turned sixteen when Ashe wins the first US Open, but he's already fearless. And that courage is matched by the confidence any impressionable youth might develop when his own mother, and a masterful psychologist like Segura, continually flatter him in a way that might seem mortifying to mere mortals. Segura doesn't mind that everyone has been saying that Jimbo is 'too small', and that he doesn't have enough of a serve. He has looked into the boy's gray eyes and recognized a 'killer'. That's what nobody else saw, the thing that would make Jimbo great. 'They didn't see that he's a killer,' he will say. 'In his head, he had everything. It didn't matter how big you were. He wasn't afraid. He could destroy you.'

Spencer Segura notices how devoted his father is becoming to his protégé. Spencer is wise beyond his years; he sees that Jimbo's slight stature and puppy-like eagerness to please — his tongue all but hangs out during practice sessions — strikes a chord with Pancho. Like him, a boy who had rickets and topped out at 5ft 6, Jimbo is more urchin than Brahmin. But Spencer also has figured out that Jimbo is no threat on the emotional front — not with Gloria and Two-Mom overwhelming him with attention and affection. With two mothers like that, who even needs a father — or a father figure?

Gloria has coupled intense training with Jimmy's indoctrination into her 'us verses them' world view. Young Jimbo's mind has been shaped like modeling clay – the teenager seems to have already deciphered that whoever will inherit the earth it certainly won't be the meek. That makes him a guy you don't want to play, for he will find and ruin you if you happen to be on the path he plans to take in his mission to conquer tennis.

It may be less than a decade since Arthur Ashe made his debut at Forest Hills, but it is a radically transformed world for tennis folks, thanks to the advent of Open tennis. Those who looked upon Gloria Connors as some sort of witch in a little white skirt as she drilled her two young boys back in East St Louis might now acknowledge that she was either prescient or damned lucky. She got a good jump on what would soon be an unfolding world of opportunity as money flowed into the game and crowds flooded tennis venues great and small, a vast migration to the sport that for so many years had been gathering dust in the closet of the public mind.

Ironically, the appeal of this emergent professional spectacle is rooted largely in its conservative nature. The public is fascinated by the rituals and discipline that shape the game – the all-white clothing, the observed silence during points, the obligatory politesse, the monochromatic ethics of that first wave of great Open-era champions of which Arthur Ashe is a part: if you're injured, you don't set foot on the court. If you set foot on the court, you aren't injured. Suddenly, Wimbledon becomes something more than yet another baffling event (like, say, Henley) on that esoteric British summer social calendar. It is now seen as a repository for some sort of buried treasure, all those rituals and orchestrated displays of manners gleaming in the summer sun like newly discovered gold doubloons from a shipwreck.

The sport is also recognized as aspirational, and this makes it newly interesting to a robust, cash-rich middle class. Take up tennis and your blood takes on a slightly bluish tint. Lords and ladies and wing commanders play tennis. The fascinating Kennedys play tennis, you know.

Yet the discipline inherent in almost everything about the sport runs counter to the spirit of the late 1960s, and the encroachment by professionalism creates a powerful inducement for those scheming to get something more than a good workout, or entrée into a coveted social set, out of tennis. There's an urgency now for those who would make a mark in the game, a compulsive rush not to be left behind as the opportunities open up.

Jimbo absorbs all the wisdom that Pancho has to offer. Day after day, the cagey old coach and his protégé sit on the veranda of this or that club, watching matches like a pair of falcons observing prey. Segura imparts wonderful tips on how to get into an opponent's head ('When you see a second serve, come in behind your return – even if the guy is coming in, too. It will tell him you aren't afraid of him, that you don't respect that serve.'). Of course, racquet science is not to be confused with rocket science, and the stratagems are useful only if the player across the net can be induced to cooperate. That may take some persuasion, which is where simple aggression comes into the picture. Segu knows this. So he keeps telling Jimbo how great he is, and he frequently and openly testifies that the floppy-haired youngster has 'big balls', bigger balls than anyone else out there. As far as advice goes, the accolade may be more valuable than all the blurred hieroglyphics on those wet cocktail napkins.

Jimbo's aggressive, athletic, all-court style begins to bear fruit quickly. By June of 1970, Connors is primed to play in the finals of the Southern California Junior Sectionals, which take place at the most storied of the SoCal tennis clubs, the Los Angeles Tennis Club. Connors' game is growing by leaps and bounds. He can't seem to get enough of the wisdom imparted by Pancho Segura, and now the other Pancho, Gonzalez. The latter was also becoming a strong influence, not least because Connors understands that Gonzalez is a fellow rebel, hard case – and showman.

In the final of the sectionals, Connors plays his doubles partner and fellow habitue of the Beverly Hills Tennis Club, Bob Kreiss. It was a relatively straightforward win for Connors (6-4, 6-2), at the expense of a friend and companion. It was said that Connors had generously awarded Kreiss a few free points out of sympathy following bad calls – at least until he grew tired of the gesture and declared: 'I can't afford to give any more free points today.' But at least one witness, a local reporter, said Connors' largesse was overstated, and the more telling detail was the way Connors swaggered around the court like he owned the place.

By the summer of that year, Jimbo is ready to break into the elite ranks. His opportunity comes at, arguably, the second most prestigious tournament in the nation, the Pacific Southwest Championships (PSW) in Los Angeles. Jimbo has just turned eighteen, and he's accepted a scholarship to play for the same school Arthur Ashe and Charlie Pasarell represented, UCLA.

Connors has not had much interaction with Ashe, although he feels a measure of respect for him. Earlier in the year at a tournament in Louisville, Eddie Dibbs had prevailed upon Jimbo to help him put black make-up on Ilie Năstase prior to a doubles match 'Nasty' was to play alongside Ashe. Jimbo was somewhat apprehensive about that stunt, but he was eager to cultivate a friendship with Năstase – the mercurial, astonishingly gifted, highly controversial Romanian. Jimbo played along and got a big kick out of the stunt. He was relieved to see that Ashe took it in his stride, laughing so hard when Năstase appeared that he all but fell over.

Not long after the US Open of 1970, Jimbo battles his way through five rounds of qualifying matches to make the main draw at the PSW, and his reward is a first-round match with the player who launched Ashe to fame, Australian veteran Roy Emerson. The prolific Grand Slam champion is older now; at the PSW tournament he is coming off a loss in the US Open doubles final, and a fourth-round singles loss to Stan Smith. Ashe then beat his friend Smith, and made it to the final – where he was upset by Năstase.

Jimbo and Segu go through a number of cocktail napkins plotting a strategy for Emerson, a superb attacker with a lethal volley. Thus, Jimbo will try to keep him away from the net and constantly moving. He will also attempt to avoid Emmo's wicked slice backhand and force him to hit low balls off his weaker, forehand wing. Connors wins the first set but when he loses the second in a tie-breaker he begins to feel the match slipping away. He reminds himself of all the generalities impressed upon him by Gloria and Segu: fear nothing. Keep the pressure on. Trust yourself. Be aggressive. Fittingly, Jimbo wins the match when he attacks Emerson's forehand once again and moves in to punch away a forehand volley.

Shortly after the match, Jimbo calls Gloria. The announcement that he has just beaten Roy Emerson is met with silence. 'Mom?' But there is still no answer. Gloria Connors is speechless.

With his reputation burgeoning, Jimbo can write his own ticket to a full scholarship at any tennis-touting university in the nation. But he has yet to read a book, and his intellectual curiosity is nonexistent. It isn't as if he has a hard time deciding between pro tennis and a career teaching the classics. Jimbo opts to remain right in the thick of things in Los Angeles, playing for Glenn Bassett at UCLA. The respected veteran coach has almost nothing to add to Jimbo's game, and understands that he'd have his fingers chopped off by Gloria if he dared tamper with it. But unlike Gloria and Segura, Bassett is plugged into the broad spectrum of athletics. He brings something valuable – and not entirely expected – to Connors' development: an almost exclusive emphasis on fitness.

Basset makes the freshman player run, and puts him through rigorous four-hour practice sessions – much longer than either Gloria or Segura feels is necessary. But those exhaustive workouts, combined with unending competition against the best upperclassmen from the finest collegiate tennis programs in the nation, improve his game even further.

In the spring, Jimbo leads UCLA to the national team title, and becomes the first freshman ever to win the singles by virtue of a hard-fought win over a junior rival and Stanford player, Roscoe Tanner.

Also in the spring, Jimbo is almost thrown out of UCLA for a startlingly brassy stunt. Since September, he's paid a down-at-the-heels senior twenty bucks a pop for term papers that he would merely have to rewrite in his own hand before turning them in. Tiring of the charade, Jimbo figures 'What the heck?' and decides that even copying the content in an acceptable manner takes too much time that could be better spent at the tennis court, or poolside. So he hands in the actual mimeographed copy of a compliant graduate student's thesis, merely scrawling his name across the top. His professor, apoplectic with rage, grabs Connors by the shirtfront, flings him against the front wall and commands him to address the class on the substance of the paper.

It's hard to say if the professor's reaction is the result of Connors having cheated – or because of the flagrant contempt in which the snot-nosed tennis player must have held the professor, and the institution, to so brazenly flout the rules.

It seems like that career in medicine or astronomy is not on the cards for Jimbo. But nothing like that will lie in store for Tanner, the beaten finalist in the 1971 NCAA, either. Although he will play a Wimbledon final and rank as high as no. 13 in the world, he will end up wearing prison stripes as a guest of the Florida Department of Corrections, and various similar agencies for, among other things, bouncing checks, failing to pay child support and felony third-degree Grand Theft charges.

*

Bill Riordan's florid face looks stove in, and he bears signs of an unsuccessful childhood battle with acne. His dark hair is thinning, gray creeping into his sideburns. He has a weak chin and crooked teeth, along with a penchant for jingling the change in the pockets of his plain and slightly rumpled gray suit. But his eyes, his watery blue eyes, dance easily and he's always up for a prank or a joke. He is a Runyonesque character shaped, partly, by early exposure to the fight game. His father had been part 'owner' of a number of prizefighters, and despite an otherwise genteel upbringing Bill whiled away many hours of his youth among the mobsters, gamblers, budding actresses and outsized characters who inhabited the smoky nether regions of Madison Square Garden on fight nights.

Riordan could easily be cast as the manager of a heavyweight palooka, but his client in his first foray into the flesh trade is the hottest young tennis player to emerge at a time when the entire world is suddenly fascinated by the game. He is the manager of Jimmy Connors.

Riordan has come a long way in the nearly two decades since he fled his native New York City, after he and his wife lost a child to a cot death. Riordan's father, the former president of Stern's, once a leading New York department store, died just six months later. A brother, Richard, ten years younger, was on the fast track to great success; he would become rich, and serve as the mayor of Los Angeles and, later, California's state Secretary of Education.

Bill was also slowly losing his battle with the bottle, and doing it with true Irish flair, his tormented soul grappling with the fun-loving, self-deprecating fatalist in him. He read Evelyn Waugh and George S. Kaufman, and was the sort of man who could peer into the dark side of life and greet it with a quip of what he sees there, a man about whom people would say, 'He's too smart for his own good.' Riordan was smoking close to three packs of cigarettes a day. Although he was a preppy and a graduate of Georgetown University, Riordan at heart was a salesman — but lacking a product in which he believed, he had nothing to sell but his own cynicism and despair.

The Riordans drifted out to Denver, then back east in 1954 to the eastern shore town of Salisbury, Maryland. With his talent for sales, Riordan could be expected to make a go of the specialty dress shop he opened. But the drinking got in the way. Finally, though, Riordan quit cold. In 1954 he flung himself, body and soul, into the sport that he had pursued in his youth alongside boxing: tennis. At the time, Salisbury had all of four courts, all of them riven with cracks sprouting weeds.

In seemingly no time at all, Riordan parlayed his role as high school tennis coach into the promoter of local junior tournaments and, later, exhibition events featuring top pros. One thing is certain: the kids love

Riordan. He is for ever pulling pranks (some of them at the expense of Salisbury's leading citizens, who often seem lacking in humor), and he becomes widely known among players for the tales he tells about a fictional player, a Polish junior champion named Stanley Stampenzak. Stanley arrived at tournaments via Air Warsaw, wearing a Nazi Second World War army helmet, prepared to deck anyone who got in his way. And so on.

By 1964, Riordan has turned Salisbury into a tennis mecca and he's assumed an important role in the establishment he always claimed to abhor, the USLTA. That same year, Riordan takes the moribund, mis-managed USLTA National Indoor tournament from New York to Salisbury and, seemingly overnight, trans-forms it into an enormous success. He does that at least in part the old-fashioned way – by ignoring the sacred laws of amateurism and joyfully greasing the palms of any player who takes the trouble to play his tournament.

For that reason, almost everyone plays. Arthur Ashe plays. He doesn't remember that it was Riordan who, years earlier, wrote him a letter explaining why his entry into a big Salisbury junior event was rejected (the theory being the real reason was not that Ashe missed the deadline, but that he was black). But Ashe will vividly remember how, when he has a good tournament in the National Indoors many years later, Riordan calls him over, extracts a 'giant wad' of bills (the only kind that a man like Riordan carries), and peels off two crisp one hundred dollar bills. Ashe would later write, 'I just didn't get that kind of payoff then; nobody did.'

When Open tennis arrives in 1968, scads of lawyers, promoters and entrepreneurs – including the likes of Donald Dell, Mark McCormack, Jack Kramer, George MacCall, Dave Dixon, Lamar Hunt and Bill Riordan – all sense that a new frontier is opening up, there to be exploited by the swiftest and strongest. There are fortunes to be made by those who create and control either the players or the tournaments or both.

The ambitions of these men could be thwarted only by each other, either individually, in alliance with each other, or in alliance with what is still the organizing force in the game, the International Lawn Tennis Federation and its various national affiliates, or federations, including the USLTA.

The power of these bodies is not God-given; it flows from their ownership rights to the four crown jewels of tennis, the Grand Slam events (strictly speaking, Wimbledon is the owner of the eponymous tournament, but the club works closely with the ITF and other three grand slams). The tennis federations and Wimbledon are not-for-profit organizations created for the express purpose of administering and popularizing the game, suddenly find themselves sitting atop four potential gold mines. The men and women who run the ILTF and its affiliates – all volunteers, engaged for the 'good of the game' – are perceived by the entrepreneurial wolves as amateurs and fuddy-duddies. But there's not much they can do about them, or about prying loose those pre-eminent major events.

Riordan, the most conspicuous lone wolf prowling this crowded and opportunity laden landscape, builds upon his success in Salisbury in the early days of Open tennis by creating the Independent Players' Association tour, which travels to small markets like Macon, Georgia, Omaha, Nebraska, and Birmingham, Alabama. Although many in the USLTA look down their noses at Riordan as a kind of blue-blood charlatan and vulgar promoter, they sagely if cynically support the IPA as a bulwark against the threat represented by men like the fabulously rich oilman and sports entrepreneur Lamar Hunt.

A founder of the American Football League, Hunt believes tennis has great potential. He wants to get players under contract to participate in a single organized league called World Championship Tennis. Hunt's rivals, and the ILTF crowd, see this as the gambit in Hunt's long-range desire to make WCT the only tennis game in town. Worse yet, most of the very top pros are lining up to sign up on Hunt's tour. That's where Jimmy Connors – and Bill Riordan – come into it.

⋆

Jimmy Connors is terrified of being drafted. He returns to UCLA in the fall of 1971, not entirely because of his love of higher learning. In school, he still has a precious student deferment that will keep him from being drafted. But late in the year he plays a Riordan event in Baltimore and reaches the final, which he loses. Soon he calls home, apologizes to Gloria, and declares that he can't pass up the money he could begin earning immediately if he quits school. Within weeks, he wins his first professional tournament, in Jacksonville, Fla. That first paycheck is for $1,500.

Shortly after, Connors is drafted. He takes his physical and is resigned to entering the army but nothing comes of it. As if by magic, the problem has gone away.

Riordan has been hovering around on the edge of the Connors family radar for some time. A charismatic 'outsider' himself, Two-Mom and Gloria take a shine to him. He seems to know all the right things to say, a category of observation that usually begins – and ends – with the fulsome praise of their son Jimmy. Riordan also knows how to fan the flames of discontent, how to remind the 'us's' that there are still plenty of 'thems' out there. But his greatest coup is convincing the women, perhaps rightly, that there's no reason for Jimbo to rush right into battle against the icons of the game. He ought to be selective, picking his spots – tournaments like those on Riordan's IPA circuit, where the competition isn't as demanding day in and day out.

Jimbo took to heart and always remembers Two-Mom's admonition that he should always keep an air of mystery about himself. This bombastic showman Riordan, who is already introducing Jimbo to others as 'the one and only Jimmy Connors', understands why that should be so. Jimbo never seemed to need a father figure – Gloria and Two-Mom more than adequately filled both roles in the parent department.

But in Riordan, Connors has found a man with whom he can bond in a way that goes deeper, if not more usefully, than the way he connects with Pancho Segura. Unlike Jimbo's indurate coach, Riordan is a sentimentalist at heart; he shamelessly compares himself and Jimmy to Butch Cassidy and the Sundance Kid. Or, as Riordan once told Curry Kirkpatrick of *Sports Illustrated*: 'Gloria and Two-Mom said how nice I was, and wouldn't it be great to have a guy like me represent a guy like Jimmy? We're generations apart, as you know, but practically the same person. The only difference is that when I started out, I made the choice between good and evil, and picked good. This kid went the other way.'

They are ready, the team is in place. Gloria, the master puppeteer, will remain in the background. Segura will handle the grunt work. With his brain in Jimbo's body, they will slaughter all rivals. Off the court, Riordan will sue the hell out of everyone.

CHAPTER SIX

Forces in Motion

'It must have really hurt Arthur to lose to Jimmy. Jimmy beat him twice in South Africa, he stole his thunder. And Jimmy was Jimmy, he's a prick, he was vulgar. It wasn't like losing to his buddy Smith. Jimmy was a punk kid who couldn't give a shit.'

Charlie Pasarell

'I later read that he [Ashe] had identified the weaknesses in my game ... Ashe's mistake was to underestimate my groundstrokes, just as he had in Boston ... That South African trip was important to me for another reason. There was no better place in the world to buy a diamond engagement ring.'

Jimmy Connors, on his trip to Johannesburg

It is a gorgeous, November day in the sunshot wine country outside of Capetown. Arthur Ashe is sitting in the courtyard of a delightful Dutch inn, under a regal, ancient oak tree, sipping tea and eating finger sandwiches. He is talking with an Afrikaner professor of anthropology named Christopf Hanekom and three of his students. Hanekom is one of the bright lights at South Africa's equivalent of Harvard, Stellenbosch University.

One of the students, a nondescript young man wearing glasses, replies to Ashe's meticulously researched statistics on the murder, rape and execution of blacks under apartheid in South Africa with a reference to the assassination of John F. Kennedy and blandly observes, with an almost rhetorical shrug, 'No system is perfect.'

Ashe, were he not so sincere and rational, might find beads of perspiration breaking out on his brow and, unwilling to stand it any more, leap to his feet and scream. There is something profoundly out of kilter about these men; they are a chilly reminder of political theorist Hannah Arendt's famous musings on 'the banality of evil'. The allegiance of these men to an unassailable brand of racism – a powerful, lethal virus born of colonialism – is not the subject of their conversation with this equally well-mannered American black man; the rightness of it has become, in their minds, the starting point for one.

'You must understand, Mr Ashe,' the professor says. 'We are different cultures [black and white], different languages, trying to find our way together. That is not an easy task.'

It never is, Ashe replies. And perhaps South Africa is not unique after all, not so different from places like Belgium, tribal Burundi, or even Canada, with its dedicated Francophone minority.

'We think we are on the road to diverse equality. A voluntary multiracialism,' the professor insists.

'We are not as static a society as it may seem,' adds the second student, a handsome, blond-haired youth with unsettlingly blue eyes. 'But at the moment we just do not believe that racial equality would benefit the whole society.'

Which 'we' would that be? Ashe replies cooly. Were the blacks in Soweto consulted? How is it justifiable that whites make all the decisions?

The South Africans allow how the condition cannot be justified except by . . . the idea of evolution.

Perhaps the Afrikaners feel that they are ganging up on this black American. They reel in their convictions a bit and, perhaps in an attempt to mollify Ashe, they point out that he, after all, is 'culturally white'.

A brief silence falls over the group. Rich afternoon light bathes the neatly tended rows of vines on the hillsides in the distance. Ashe does not want to go on with the conversation. He does not really want to engage in the self-inflicted humiliation that will unavoidably attend his final plea. He will ask them to set aside all their theories and philosophy, look inside themselves and ask: 'Is it right?'

He does not want to do that because no spectacle is more dispiriting than seeing that which is right groveling before that which is powerful. But he will do it. He will do it because he is Arthur Ashe Jr.

Arthur Ashe first applies for a visa to visit South Africa in 1969. His awareness of race — and race relations — has been maturing right along with his tennis game. Ashe wants to see the apartheid system, the notoriety of which seems to be growing daily, with his own eyes. He wants to make his own judgements about it before he begins to take a public position on what certainly seems like a cruel, inhumane and racist form of social organization and governance. His application is turned down.

The previous year, while Ashe was still at West Point, he had spent much time in the winter in the weight room. As a boy in Richmond, had been taunted and teased about his physique and his legs were so spindly and knees so knobby that he dreaded the days when he was obliged to wear shorts pants for gym. At the US Military Academy he became so ripped and felt so confident in this newer, stronger version of himself it may have played a role in his decision to make a strong speech about racial inequality. For that he was summoned to the office of the chief of staff, where he was informed that as an officer in the US Army he was forbidden to speak harshly of his country.

But Ashe completed his military obligations shortly thereafter, and a few months later he won the US Open. Then, in 1969, he amassed an outstanding win–loss record of 72–10, and won ten of the twenty-two tournaments he entered. He also led the US to a successful defense of the Davis Cup, winning both his singles matches against Romania in the Challenge Round. In early 1970, Ashe added a second Grand Slam title, that of the Australian Open, to his résumé. He was twenty-seven years old and at, or near, the peak of his powers.

Connors is just eighteen in 1970, and soon to join Ashe on the roll of UCLA men who had won the prestigious NCAA singles title. But the mad rush to professionalism, combined with the particular genius of Connors, are rapidly shrinking time in terms of his development. Before long, the idea that a player might not want or have to play against the absolute best in the world on a regular basis until well past the age of twenty-one would be unthinkable. For Connors, though, it was a sound strategy.

Shortly after he turns pro in 1972, Connors is called up for Davis Cup duty (he had been a practice partner on the squad in 1971). He's never been terribly interested in the competition. His reserves of patriotism seem easily exhausted and, besides, the pay is lousy (playing Davis Cup is seen as a form of national service, and payback to the national federations). But Connors agrees to accompany the US squad to Jamaica – where he finds himself sitting on the bench as the singles assignments are doled out to two clearly weaker players – Erik van Dillen, the 'golden boy' who never panned out as a singles player, and Tom Gorman.

The theory in the Connors camp back in Salisbury and St Louis is that team captain Dennis Ralston – who is represented by Dell – is playing politics. It is one of the many examples Riordan and others will cite when they accuse Dell of being power hungry, and bent on dominating the game. In Jamaica, Connors is stewing in his own juices as he prepares, with teeth gritted, to play the role of cheerleader and orange peeler for the singles stars.

But before the final day of play, when Connors is penciled in to play one of the dead rubbers following a 3-0 sweep by the US, Gloria Connors calls and tersely tells Jimbo that there is a problem at home. She wants him to return to Los Angeles – immediately. He does not ask why; he just does as he's told. But he gradually fills with dread. When his connecting flight to Los Angeles is delayed, he calls Gloria and learns that Two-Mom has died of a heart attack.

Jimbo is so shaken by the news, so bitterly disappointed that Two-Mom has been taken from him just as he's about to cash in and get her comfortably settled on Easy Street, that he decides to quit the game. He tells Gloria that he's going back to school. Gloria reminds him that Two-Mom loved nothing more than tennis, and that she dedicated her life to it partly to give Jimbo every possible opportunity to succeed.

After Jimbo mulls over Gloria's words, and spends some time grieving for the woman who provided the notes that he tucked into his socks and pulled out to read during changeovers, he decides to continue playing tennis. But the tragedy, combined with the snub by Ralston, leaves a bad taste in Connors' mouth so powerful that it will be years before he even considers playing Davis Cup again – and it won't end well then, either.

The death of Two-Mom has another significant outcome. She had always been a credible and effective counterweight to her obsessive, mistrustful, jealousy prone daughter Gloria. She was the good cop to Gloria's bad cop, and Gloria certainly listened to her in matters as diverse as the way Jimmy hit his forehand to the family's embrace of Segura and Riordan. With Two-Mom gone, there is no longer any curb on Gloria's most compulsive instincts, nor any voice to tell her nobody is going to rob her of her son, or steal the credit she deserves as his creator.

The landscape in 1972, year five of the Open era, is chaotic, verging on anarchic. Competing promoters are operating different tours while the establishment, which consists of the International Lawn Tennis Federation and its affiliates, are deathly afraid that the professionals and their aggressive agents will hijack the game and destroy the system and traditions they've created. These fears are stoked by the changing nature of the tennis audience. Tennis suddenly trembles on the threshold of hipness, and it is attracting a new type of fan as controversial, outspoken, expressive players like Connors, the notorious Pancho Gonzalez, Ilie Năstase and (soon) John McEnroe generate headlines.

The typical tennis fan has always been well-educated if not necessarily wealthy, perhaps with an air of the connoisseur about him. A good deal of tennis's appeal is rooted in the personalities of the players. The last great generation of amateurs was from Australia, and personified by Rod Laver. These men largely were tight-lipped, understated and disciplined; they were hard cases who eschewed emotional demonstrations. But the advent of professionalism creates unprecedented diversity among the players as well as the fans. The money in the game lures players from far and wide; many do not subscribe to the Anglo-based codes of conduct and sportsmanship. At the same time, the fans are increasingly interested in people; it's the dawn of the age of celebrity. And no sport delivers people in as accessible and vulnerable a way as tennis. There are no helmets to hide the face, the men wear shorts and the women skimpy dresses or skirts. Fans comfortably call their favorites by their given names, as if they were long-standing friends.

Fans have always turned out to see famous tennis players like Big Bill Tilden, Suzanne Lenglen, or Fred Perry. They, and others like them, achieved celebrity status long before the Open era. But in the new age, people flock to tennis tournaments not just because they want to see tennis played by those rare transcendent stars, but because they themselves want to be seen. Large numbers of new fans don't buy tickets because they want to see the game; they plonk down their pounds and dollars and francs because they want to experience and be part of the glamour associated with the game and the clubs where the tournaments are played. People feel much more comfortable expressing their feelings on the heels of the sixties; they are more inclined to choose favorites and heroes. They are seduced like never before, by the anti-hero. Tennis is no longer a contest between two players with matching skill sets. It is often seen as a confrontation between different personalities, and it's all right to express your own preference. You could be a Rolling Stones person or a Beatles person, but not really both. You could be a Năstase person or a Laver person, but not really both.

By 1972, the political struggle between the ILTF and WCT is so intense that thirty-two players on WCT professional tour are barred from playing at the French Open and Wimbledon. And worse is to come. But Riordan and Connors thrive under these chaotic conditions. Ashe, Cliff Drysdale, Charlie Pasarell and others, advised and in many cases represented by Dell, want to bring greater organization into the game. They have one foot in the old world and one in the new. They don't want tennis to morph into a circus; at the same time, they are in the process of forming the players' union that will come to be known as the Association of Tennis Professionals. Riordan wants no part of it, and Connors will become the only top player to shun the organization.

Riordan expertly uses Connors as a wedge against opposing forces represented by men like World Championship Tennis kingpin Lamar Hunt and Riordan's main tormentor, Donald Dell. As manager of the top American players, including Ashe and Stan Smith, Dell is becoming the most powerful man in the evolving pro game. Riordan is turning himself into a power broker in his own right by denying Dell the cooperation of the most electric talent to come of age in the early Open era, and by building strong relations with the USLTA. That organization sees Riordan's Independent Players' Association as a proxy in the fight against World Championship Tennis. The very name IPA is a dig at those players who had signed contracts to play on the WCT tour, thereby allegedly sacrificing their 'independence'.

Meanwhile, Jimbo cleans up on the IPA tour. It isn't merely because Connors is up against men who, were they boxers, would fall into the category of 'tomato cans'. The tour also features Ilie Năstase and a host of other quality players who give Connors plenty of competition. Năstase, in fact, dominates Connors on the court, but at least Jimbo doesn't have to suffer the indignity of getting whipped in the first or second round, week after week, by a Ken Rosewall, a Rod Laver – or an Arthur Ashe.

The top pros accuse Connors of ducking the competition. They are dying to get at him, punk that he is, and in the echo chamber there is little room for the voice cautioning, 'Be careful what you wish for.' The growing enmity isn't helped by the fact that Riordan expresses nothing but contempt for all those vetted champions who have waited so long for the chance to play Open tennis, and who now see Connors and Riordan as agents who would keep the game from evolving in a way that preserves many of its traditional features.

And all the while, Riordan keeps banging the drum and twisting the knife, 'With Jimmy, sometimes it was like leading a symphony,' he would say. 'And I don't believe anyone could have done it like Connors. He never deviated from the script I wrote him.'

The rift between Connors and the players grows deeper, accelerated by his increasingly controversial, unsportsmanlike antics. Ilie Năstase, the Romanian bad boy, has become an unlikely role model for the impressionable Midwesterner. Even when he is losing to Nasty, Connors is learning – and not necessarily about tennis. He can ape all of Nasty's moves, and adds some of his own. Jimbo pirouettes around, limp-wristed, when he misses an easy shot. He hurls obscenities. He clutches his private parts, or suggestively strokes the handle of his racquet. He points at opponents and wags his finger when they dare make a good shot or question a line call. When the charismatic Năstase does such things, he seems merely sophomoric. But sometimes Connors' theatrics come across as somehow vulgar – the sort of behaviour capable of making some people avert their eyes, and draw their daughters closer for protection.

Thriving on the attention, Connors mouths off like a punk in a poorly written B-movie. 'I know what the others say, but I'm not that obnoxious,' he tells *Sports Illustrated*'s Curry Kirkpatrick. 'I am not a punk. I'm 5-10, 155 pounds. I've got broad shoulders and I can pack a punch. Most of these guys are windbags anyway. If they ever try anything with me, I'll be over the net – fast.'

Jimbo is displeased with the story Kirkpatrick writes. Shortly after it appears, he tells me that when it comes to future dealings with *Sports Illustrated*, 'I wouldn't give them the sweat off my balls.'

The separate tributaries representing the careers of Arthur Ashe and Jimmy Connors begin to flow in increasing proximity in 1973. By this time, twenty-one-year-old Connors is ready for a major breakout while Ashe, approaching thirty, is immersing himself more and more deeply into politics: those of tennis and those of race. He is becoming a spokesperson on both fronts.

Connors reaches the final of all eight tournaments he plays in the run-up to the French Open, winning six of those titles. Ashe, signed with WCT, plays thirteen tournaments over the same four-and-three-quarter-month period, thanks to the robust indoor schedule of the elite tour. He reaches the finals six times but wins only once. He is denied the chance to play at Wimbledon, where his powerful serve and willingness to volley are well suited to the grass courts, because of a seminal event in the evolution of the game, the Wimbledon boycott of 1973.

The conflict is just the latest, but the most crucial, in a series of skirmishes between the players and the ILTF establishment. It occurs because the tennis federation of what was then the nation of Yugoslavia has asked Wimbledon to bar ATP founding member Niki Pilić from playing in London because Pilić chose to play in a tournament in Canada instead of a Davis Cup tie. He was punished with a suspension. Rules stipulate that players who are not in 'good standing' with their national associations become ineligible to compete in ITLF events. Wimbledon feels duty-bound to honor the request.

As a result, seventy of the top players, including defending champion Stan Smith, Arthur Ashe, John Newcombe, Ken Rosewall and others vote to walk out. Jimmy Connors is not one of them. Later he would brag:

'By the end of 1974 ninety-nine out of the top one hundred players were ATP members. Guess who the exception was?' In Rome, a few weeks before Wimbledon, ATP president Cliff Drysdale sought out Connors to explain the developing situation and to ask for his support; Connors said he'd get back to Cliff on it. He never did.

A few other top players, including Connors' pal Năstase, Alex Metreveli of the Soviet Union, and Czechoslovakia's Jan Kodeš, also refuse to join the boycott. They claim that the all-powerful federations in their authoritarian Communist countries ordered them to play. But the opportunity for the handful of elite players capable of winning the event creates so much pressure that neither Connors nor Năstase lasts beyond the quarter-finals.

Later that summer, the inevitable comes to pass. Connors will play Ashe in the final of the US Pro Championships in Boston, for long the premier tourna-ment for pros excluded from amateur-only events. For that reason, it rivals the Pacific Southwest Championships as the most important tournament out-side the Grand Slams.

The match is played on a Monday night, under lights. It lasts three hours and ten minutes and five sets. Ashe never feels he's playing well, but that may be because Segura – who knows his game well – loaded up Connors with sound advice. He told Jimbo that he had to rattle the quiet, confident Ashe. He advised Jimbo to return hard and deep down the middle. He reminded him to cut off the angles available to Ashe, who is dangerous when free to slash at the ball and go for the impressive placement.

The tactics paid off; Connors won in five sets, 6-3, 4-6, 6-4, 3-6, 6-2. Ashe walked off the court with an even greater appreciation of the pace and penetration of Connors' groundstrokes. But, having had a break point that might have reversed the outcome early in the fifth set, Ashe felt that his own strategy of keeping the ball down the middle to dampen the effects of his opponent's counterpunching, combined with a focus on attacking Connors' relatively weak second serve, was the correct template.

The loss brought Ashe's record in finals in 1973 to 1-8, and while he found that disturbing he had other things on his mind. He was awaiting the disposition of the South African government on his third application for a visa to visit that country and play in an ATP tennis tournament there. On the night of 31 October – Halloween – he received the news that his visa application had been accepted.

It tends to dilute what has become an inspirational story, but the decision to issue Ashe a visa was not entirely the product of Pretoria's willingness to engage with liberal forces or Ashe's sterling character and powers of persuasion. It might not have happened at all were it not for the advent of Open tennis. The Johannesburg tournament is part of the 'Grand Prix' that links all the ATP-sanctioned tournaments. Should an ATP player (one soon destined to become the outfit's president, in fact) be barred from playing in an ATP event, the organization would almost be obliged to withdraw its sanction – leaving South Africa, where tennis is enormously popular, without a pro men's tournament. Any number of white South Africans might not like that idea, whatever their feelings about apartheid.

Arthur Ashe has been pulled in different directions ever since he's been more willing to express his opinions and attitudes. Perhaps regrettably, almost all the efforts to draw him out in that way have had to do with race relations – sometimes in absurdly tangential ways. Billie Jean King, for instance, the firebrand and activist, was so incensed by Ashe's refusal to buy into her feminist agenda that she cruelly suggested that she was more 'black' than Arthur Ashe. It was a cheap shot that must have hurt, but a blow that Ashe absorbed in his familiar, stoic way.

Now he has pulled off a coup of sorts, securing a visa to visit and play pro tennis in Johannesburg, South Africa. In what is becoming a familiar pattern, parties criticize him for engaging with the South African government while others in almost equal measure believe that his visit will help focus the attention of the world on the horrors of apartheid, and perhaps even accelerate its demise.

Before Ashe leaves, his manager Donald Dell warns him: 'Arthur, nobody's going to listen to a losing quarter-finalist.' It's a harsh but realistic assessment from a man who is rapidly becoming much more than a manager.

From the moment Ashe arrives in South Africa, his mind, senses and emotions are under constant bombardment. Is the mustachioed customs official who examines his passport giving him a look, or is he just one of those intense human beings? Ashe and his party (which consists of *Sports Illustrated* writer Frank Deford and the Dells, Donald and his wife Carole) will stay in the best part of town. They're driven there by a man sympathetic to the anti-apartheid movement, the affable and popular tournament director Owen Williams. Looking out the car window, Ashe sees nothing different from what he might observe if they were rolling through Westchester County, New York.

This is a preview of what will become a familiar dilemma for Ashe. South Africa appears to be full of folks, seemingly good folks, who profess to abhor apartheid, but here they are and here is apartheid, too. Ashe is too reasonable and well-intentioned a man to revile those South African liberals whose stake in the system prevents them from throwing their full weight behind change. He just hopes they can continue to work for the greater long-term good.

When Ashe is settled into his house, that of a wealthy young Jewish lawyer, recently divorced, he sits down to lunch with a large party of friends and supporters. He politely asks for a cold drink. The maid lowers her eyes and says, 'Yes, master.'

It will go on like this, Ashe ever aware of the chilling ironies (he is, after all, a black man himself) and double standards, legal and otherwise, everywhere he turns. He will experience wild fluctuations of emotion, moved nearly to tears of joy by the smile of a black child clutching a tennis racquet, driven to the verge of anguish by the bland justifications and rationalizations offered up by so many men and women who – and this may be the worst part – actually mean well and thus cannot be simply hated or ignored by Ashe.

By agreement with the South African government, he will refrain from criticizing the government or system while he is a guest. This calls for some tricky rhetorical moves in his press conferences and interactions with officials and the media in general. But Ashe is more than up to the job. Visiting Soweto, he has to bite his lip. The district seems more of an urban reservation for the impoverished than a neighborhood.

Other experiences bring Ashe to the brink of vertigo. In addition to having a tail (presumably an agent of the government), Ashe is one day followed while walking in the city by a young African boy. When Ashe finally stops and asks the kid what he is doing, the child replies that he just wants to see what a free black man looks like. When Ashe spots his first 'Whites Only' sign before a rest room he is horrified to feel happy, in much the same way a tourist in Paris feels gratified when he finally lays his eye on the Eiffel Tower. One billboard at the tennis stadium, an advertisement for Scotch whiskey, proclaims 'Time to Serve Black and White'. Ashe takes note.

This is an enormous learning experience for Ashe, and his schedule is so loaded and his mind so preoccupied with the great social and political issues that he might easily forget he still has a tennis tournament to play – and that nobody listens to losing quarter-finalists. It's a slightly different kind of tennis tournament, too, and not just because of its location. Ellis Park, the site of the South African Open, stands at an altitude of 1,753m (5, 751ft). The air is so thin that after his first practice session Ashe resolves to get an oxygen tank to use courtside on changeovers.

Sherwood Stewart, a friendly, popular pro from Goose Creek, Texas, is the no. 36 singles player in the US (his genius is for doubles), and he's flown halfway around the globe to play in Jo'burg. He wants to be present as Ashe makes history. He will get to witness that event all right, and in the best possible way – as Ashe's first-round opponent. Learning this, Ashe smiles and says to no one in particular: 'I came all the way to Jo'burg and how do I make history? I play a guy from Goose Creek, Texas.'

Jimmy Connors is also playing in South Africa, although for radically different reasons from Ashe. He's looking to score a humongous diamond ring to present, along with a marriage proposal, to his girlfriend, eighteen-year-old fellow pro Chris Evert. He's heard that you can get a great deal on a diamond in South Africa. The exotic location also offers a welcome respite from the inordinate amount of attention that began to fall upon the couple shortly after they began dating, just before the 1972 Wimbledon tournament.

The two first met many years earlier, when the Connors prevailed upon the Everts to give them a ride at a junior tournament. And Gloria Connors had briefly dated Chris's father, teaching pro Jimmy Evert, when he was at Notre Dame University. The youngsters found themselves at a banquet a few weeks before Wimbledon in 1972, and within days Jimbo called to ask for a date. By then, Evert had already been dubbed 'the Ice Maiden' for her extraordinary composure on the tennis court. Over time, though, she would become just 'Chrissie'.

Jimbo took Chrissie on a first date to a popular steak house in London's Carlton Tower Hotel. Then he escorted her to the Playboy Club, a place Jimbo found so awesome that even in middle age, while describing the beautiful women and blackjack and craps tables, he would ask: 'Does life get any better than that?' He would also brag how, after a night full of kissing and giggling and teenage hijinks he 'played the gentleman' and settled for a kiss goodnight instead of demanding casual sex.

Well, that 'gentleman' act didn't last very long, by mutual consent. After all, these were youngsters with supercharged hormones. Besotted by the time Wimbledon was concluded (Chrissie made the semis, Jimbo the quarters), the two made no secret about being head over heels in love, and they soon became the favorites of the paparazzi.

Evert graduated from St Thomas Aquinas High School in Fort Lauderdale in June 1973. Chrissie's parents, Jimmy and Colette Evert, were conservative Catholics. They had forbidden Chris to travel alone, but when she realized after the US Open of 1973 that she might not see Jimbo for months she rebelled. She wrote her parents a note and caught a flight to Los Angeles. Her parents softened. They allowed her to travel without Colette as long as she was accompanied by either her sister, Jeanne, or her best friend, Ana Leaird.

While Ashe is busy debating the nature of apartheid, fending off charges of being an 'Uncle Tom' (that, from Africans) or fielding accolades as a potential force for the good of Africa, Jimbo is ruining reputations – and not just Chrissie's. He's savaging opponents, left and right, tournament after tournament.

The South African Open, despite being a one-week event with a draw of thirty-two, uses the best of five sets format. In his first three matches, all straight sets wins, Jimbo gives up more than four games in just one set – he won that one, 7-5. This brings him into the semi-finals, and a match with one of Ashe's friends, Tom Okker. 'The Flying Dutchman' manages to wrestle a set from Connors, but the match isn't really close. When Okker leaves the court he is almost physically shaken. He tells Ashe, 'Nobody has ever played better tennis against me.'

Given the way Connors is playing, Ashe can count himself lucky to be in the other half of the draw. Yet he isn't particularly intimidated. He looks back on their first meeting, earlier that year in Boston, as a missed opportunity. For one thing, Ashe wears glasses. The Boston final was played at night, outdoors, under what he thought was inadequate lighting. This match will be an entirely different thing. For another, Ashe never felt like he played his best tennis that night, yet the match went to five sets and Ashe squandered a chance to go a break up in the fifth. Ashe believes he was on the right track in that match – strategy and tactic wise – but then Connors did as well, and for a superior reason. He won.

The final leaves little doubt about which man's optimism was more justified. During the match Ashe's fans in the standing-room only crowd are so enthusiastic on his behalf that he pleads with them not to applaud his opponent's errors. Regrettably for Ashe, those are too few and far between. Sneering and snarling, entitled for once to truly feel like at an outsider at this lovefest for Ashe, Connors once again puts into play the tactics Segura devised, starting with the dictum to hit the ball very hard, right down the middle. Connors wins with relative ease, 6-4, 7-6, 6-3.

After the match, Ashe concedes that Connors' sheer firepower off the ground — his typical forehands and backhands — were more lethal than he expected, an odd confession given that the two had played before. But Ashe also feels that he more or less held his own — that things easily might have been different had he done this or that a little differently, or at a different time. Connors' win is more convincing than the earlier one, and he will leave Jo'burg feeling good about his game, but still a little miffed at the extent to which Ashe had underestimated his groundstrokes. It was almost insulting.

But why dwell on the negative? Jimbo has just won the tournament — as has his traveling companion and girlfriend, Evert. In the women's final, Evert defeated her young rival, pure-blooded Australian Aborigine Evonne Goolagong. Just why Goolagong's presence did not cause a stir comparable to the one Ashe created is a mystery best left to the ages. It may have had something to do with the fact that Goolagong was traveling under the wing and watchful, controlling eye of her surrogate father and mentor, lilywhite Aussie tennis coach Vic Edwards.

Afterward, Jimbo takes Chrissie to visit a diamond mine, where he uses part of his tournament earnings to buy a ring. He drops to one knee right then and there and proposes marriage as he slips the ring on her finger. The trip has been a success, in more ways than one. When Chrissie returns home, Colette Evert immediately espies the rock glimmering on her finger. All she can say is, 'I don't think you should let your father see that. Don't you think he and Jimmy should talk first?'

CHAPTER SEVEN

Reaping the Whirlwind

'Don't tell me about Arthur Ashe. Christ, I'm blacker than Arthur Ashe.'

Billie Jean King

'One of the first times I met Jimmy was in Nice. Harold Solomon was there too. One day we were outside and Solly [Solomon] comes out of the room and tells Jimmy that he has a phone call from his mother. Jimmy says, "Oh thanks." We're still by the door when he gets on and says, "Hi, Mommy! Hi, Daddy!" And then he starts talking baby talk. Really. I'll never forget that as long as I live.'

Stan Smith

Arthur Ashe Jr walks in the woods near his childhood home in Richmond, Virginia, on 9 December 1973. It sounds as if he is treading on potato chips because the leaves shed by the hardwoods are all crunchy due to a heavy overnight frost. Ashe hunkers down in the position he's been assigned, clutching a shotgun. It is still and cold, but as the sun breaks over the nearby hills and warms the ground tendrils of mist rise from the forest floor.

He is one of about twenty men who are spaced evenly in a semi-circle covering a large area. About five of these men, including his father, are black. The rest are white. Arthur Jr is thirty years old, and he marvels at how much change the past two decades have wrought. He has been fishing and hunting with his father, a devoted outdoorsman, since he was a young shaver. But never before has he shared the company of white men on a deer hunt, as he is now doing.

Suddenly, he hears a crashing in the woods. The dogs, trained to drive deer to the men, are doing their work. Then a deer is darting and leaping through the woods, toward Arthur. As the hunter brings the shotgun up he hears a shot from off to his right. At the same moment, he feels a sharp sting in the inside of his left thigh and instantly knows he knows he's been shot. But, concentrating on the task at hand, he sights down the barrel of the shotgun. He squeezes the trigger and touches off a shot. The deer stumbles and falls dead.

The projectile that hit Ashe in the leg is not really a bullet but a pellet of 'buckshot' (so named for the obvious reason), fired just moments before Ashe discharged his own weapon. The pellet didn't even penetrate the pants, but Arthur's leg is bleeding a little and it hurts like all get out. This is not a life-threatening injury.

As the flurry of action dies down and the dogs appear, their tongues lolling out the sides of their mouths, a number of the men, including both Arthurs, stand over the deer and relive the hunt. By now the sun has cleared the treetops. It warms the shoulders of the men in their red and black woolen jackets and canvas jeans. The deer needs to be field dressed – slit open from the genitals to the ribcage, all the guts and organs cut loose and pulled out. It's messy work that leaves the man doing it covered in blood up to the elbows and the dogs excited by the prospect of fresh viscera and meat.

As the man who made the killing shot, Arthur Ashe Jr gets the largest and choicest portion of the meat – a hindquarter. The Ashes linger, talking with their fellow hunters for a bit, and then shake hands and go their separate ways. On his way home, Arthur Jr wonders why he still takes such deep satisfaction and pride in having done his bit to put meat on the table. He is world-famous and rich now. He is much-loved and respected. He travels the world, staying in the finest hotels and eating in the best restaurants – all because he is uncommonly good at a simple game.

Ashe has not forgotten or lost interest in the activities he grew up with, the things that were drilled into him by his father. His love of the outdoor pursuits is one of those things, as is his conviction that you owe a hard day's work for a good day's pay – that you feel fully a man when you are able to put meat on the table.

Sometimes it all seems too much for Ashe – especially when it comes to his status as a black champion in an overwhelmingly white sport. The British generally think he's insufficiently radical, a lofty position easily touted from the safety of a redoubt across an ocean. To many whites in the US, Ashe is too radical – as demonstrated by his increasing activism regarding apartheid. The conflicts and mixed emotions are only exacerbated by what otherwise might be called the privileges of his position.

Earlier in 1973, Ashe wrote in his diary: 'Just look at me: at the same time that I got turned away from a public movie theater [for being black], I was treated royally at the most exclusive country clubs in the United States. We [players] all learned to expect to be catered to. We were put up at a magnificent estate, somebody's teen-age daughter or friend drove us around at our beck and call, we ate at the house or signed checks at the club, played golf at the club, and got invited to all the tennis-week parties.'

At the time, the pro tour often stopped at River Oaks, a posh country club which was at that time seemingly reserved for the leading white families of Houston, Texas. During Ashe's stint with World Championship Tennis, River Oaks renovated the main clubhouse and then surprisingly decreed that the visiting pro players would not be invited to make use of it. The leading players, including Australia's Fred Stolle, speculated that the rule was implemented in order to keep Ashe out of the clubhouse. They had a quick meeting, and resolved that unless the players – all of them – could use the clubhouse they would not compete in the tournament at all.

Stolle would later tell me: 'At the time, the players also were "auctioned" off, or sold, on the night before the tournament. It was something for charity, to see whose player won the tournament. It was just part of the fun. When it came to selling Arthur, well . . . there was a certain amount of coughing and shuffling of feet but Arthur, he took it right in stride. He knew the intent. He even made a joke: "Here we go again. I'm being sold as a slave."'

On the tour, Ashe plays tennis with – and against – a number of South Africans, including Ray Moore and a man who would become a close friend, Cliff Drysdale. He knows them to be good men. Some other people Arthur knows and even admires would just as soon toss a cup of animal blood at the likes of Moore and Drysdale as shake hands with them.

Ashe's role straddling two worlds, and trying his level best to reconcile them in his own mind as well as in the eyes of the world, exacts a terrible emotional price. It's draining work, and it has only gotten worse as adulthood has shaped Ashe's intellect and heightened his awareness of, among other things, leadership, responsibility – and irony.

Billie Jean King, the activist for equal pay for women tennis pros, tried to recruit Ashe to her cause. He won't join her fight; after thinking through it all, he just doesn't feel the women deserve the same amount of prize money. Ashe is convinced that paying customers plonk down their pounds or dollars at Wimbledon or the US Open mainly to watch the men who, undoubtedly, are bigger, faster, stronger – and play a more compelling game. King is so contemptuous of Ashe that she makes a remark she will regret, snapping, 'I'm blacker than Arthur Ashe.'

If the remark angers or hurts Ashe, he's careful not to show it. But of course it does sting him; many things of this nature do. By the age of thirty he has come to a realization: 'The first twenty-five years of my life whites were telling me what to do, then the next years blacks began telling me what to do. When do we get to the point where Arthur Ashe tells Arthur Ashe what to do?'

But pulled and torn as he is, Ashe's dilemma seldom influenced his outlook, or his opinion of his fellow man. He struggles not to become a cynic with signature success. However, his increasing awareness of the ironies attending his life seems to have an impact on his tennis. By the end of July 1973, he has lost seven of his last eight finals – including the match that Jimmy

Connors himself would come to describe as his transilient moment.

Many years later, when tennis would be the least of Ashe's concerns (albeit one of his abiding loves), he will write: 'All I know is that I have tried at all times to do what I thought was right and appropriate, and that sometimes the effort to do right, and above all not to do wrong, led me to inaction.' And he would tell a reporter from *People* magazine, sent to do a story on how he was coping with AIDS, 'You're not going to believe this, but being black is the greatest burden I've had to bear.'

One person who wasn't about to believe that Ashe could say such a thing is his steadfast manager, Donald Dell. That final quotation makes sensational headlines. When Dell, in Munich, Germany, on business is read the quotation by an associate, he calls Ashe in the middle of the night, asking if he was quoted accurately.

'Donald,' Ashe says. 'We've never really gotten into it on this kind of thing. You're not black. What you don't understand is that I'm fine. I do better in a white world in a lot of ways. I've benefited from being black in a white sport. But I have to adjust every single day how I act in a certain environment depending on who is there. If it's all white, one way; country club, another way; all black, a third way. I have to adjust my thinking or behavior or response every day.'

But in mid-1974, Ashe had pressing professional

concerns to address as well. In a reprise of his struggles in early 1973, Ashe fails to win a final in four tries starting in mid-April. Only two of those finals are against fellow Grand Slam champions (Björn Borg and John Newcombe). The word on the tennis street is that at the age of thirty-plus, the two-time Grand Slam champion might never win another big match – not with the likes of Borg coming of age, and the game held in a death grip by the electric, controversial American, Jimbo Connors.

Verily, she hath prophesied that their enemies shall reap the whirlwind; her son the outsider would smite them, one and all, and there would be much weeping and gnashing of teeth throughout the kingdom among those who would stand in their way, or challenge the righteousness of their cause or their thirst for retribution and vengeance. And these prognostications all come to pass in the year of vindication, the year of our Lord, 1974.

Together, Jimbo and Gloria would conquer and sub-jugate the whole of tennis in a great unleashing of bitter force accumulated through long years of toil, sacrifice and obsessional ambition. It's a long time coming, yet when the moment was ripe the proph-ecy comes to fruition as precipitate as a summer thunderstorm.

Jimbo made his first mark among the best players in the world in 1970, with that win over aging Roy Emerson in the Pacific Southwest Championships. From there, the process accelerated. By the time rivals and observers came to grips with just how good he was, Jimbo was already better — always one step ahead of the game. By early 1972, Connors felt himself ready to sever ties with the amateur and collegiate games.

In his own mind, Connors established himself as the champion of the future at the prestigious US Pro Championships of 1973. In the first round, he demolished the top player in the world, Stan Smith. Three impressive wins later, he found himself in the final, once again across the net from Arthur Ashe.

After losing that match, Ashe would — somewhat cavalierly — write in his diary, 'We went three hours and ten minutes and five sets, and still, I hardly ever felt that I was playing well. Sometimes I thought I was just lucky to be out there, but we were dead even for four sets and I had an [advantage] on Connors serve in the first game of the fifth set, and if I win that one point I'm up a break, and maybe I run the whole thing out.'

Connors won it, 6-3, 4-6, 6-4, 3-6, 6-2. He had his own reasons for taking particular satisfaction in the biggest win of his career to that point. He was aware that some members of the press had taken to describing him as being just 'Chris Evert's boyfriend'. After the win, he said, 'Screw 'em, I'm starting to make my own name now.'

Almost exactly two years after he accepted his first official professional prize-money check, Jimbo becomes a Grand Slam champion with a win at the Australian Open of 1974. He is obliged to beat four Australians along the way. In his final two matches he successively topples John Alexander and Phil Dent, a brace of Aussies who are expected to carry on the great winning tradition established by the likes of Sedgman, Hoad, Rosewall and Laver. It is yet another warning shot fired across the bow of the establishment.

Between early January and April of 1974, Connors wins seven of the eight tournaments he enters, and loses in the final of the eighth. Yet the skeptics dwell on the fact that these are the 'Riordan tour' events, played in podunk towns like Omaha, Nebraska; Birmingham, Alabama; and Tempe, Arizona. Neither Jimbo nor his management team minds that. Jimbo is gorging on victories, building confidence and self-esteem. He likes the smell and taste of blood. He's ferret-like, eager to dig a player, any player, out of whatever hole he enters – be it in Salt Lake City, Utah, or in some major state capital. Connors' intensity is such that he easily loses himself in the task at hand. When he looks up for a moment during a match, his eyes are bright and shining and you half expect to see a halo of blood surrounding his mouth.

All the publicity showered upon the 'love doubles' match of Evert and Connors, combined with Jimbo's increasingly impressive résumé, makes him famous. He feels like 'a movie star' when he enters a restaurant with his idol-turned-wingman, Ilie Năstase. They sometimes receive an ovation and best wishes from their fellow diners. Connors feels like he might be king of the world, even if Gloria doesn't approve of either Evert or Năstase. Each, in his and her own way, appears to be a threat to the Connors' ambitions – aspirations so intricately interwoven that it's impossible to distinguish those of one from those of the other.

Jimbo's burgeoning reputation earns him a lucrative offer from the Baltimore Banners, a franchise of a new tennis enterprise called World Team Tennis. He has also inked a deal with a perfume maker that would pay him a windfall should he win all four major (Grand Slam) events in 1974. Completing this 'Grand Slam' is considered the highest achievement in tennis, and has been accomplished by only two men – Donald Budge and Rod Laver.

WTT is an attempt to turn tennis into a city-based team sport, like football, or basketball. Open tennis, embraced in 1968, energized and accelerated a 'tennis boom' and that attracted entrepreneurs and promoters of every stripe, many of them hell-bent on inventing the better mouse trap. Billie Jean King's husband, Larry, is one of the main forces behind WTT. The architects of this league believe that tennis would really prosper if only it could shed many of its traditional components – elements that at the moment were making it wildly popular. Over time they would pay a serious price for this obvious miscalculation.

But in 1974, numerous players are seduced by the largesse of the WTT owners. It's crazy money the ego-driven owners are throwing around. But also, the idea of playing an abbreviated, team-based version of the game while having a home base for a few weeks has a measure of appeal. Enough of the top players express an interest in playing WTT that the establishment feels the tournament game is threatened. Philippe Chatrier, one of the great visionaries in the establishment, is particularly disturbed by the way the creators of WTT, in setting their spring season, show flagrant disregard for the rich history of the European clay-court circuit.

Declaring war on the upstart WTT, Chatrier announces that anyone who participates in the league (which has franchises only in the US) would be barred from the French Open. Both Australian Open champions, Connors and Evonne Goolagong, are immediately subject to the ban. Bill Riordan, Connors' manager, files a legal claim to have Connors' ban overturned on the grounds that it unlawfully prevents him from pursuing his profession. Also, by denying him the right to play a Grand Slam event (the French Open), Connors is prevented from earning that great perfume company payout.

The law is unsympathetic. It rules against Riordan and Connors, who merely shrugs and considers the dispute ended. Connors misses the French Open, and turns his attention to Wimbledon – where he is not banned. When he arrives in London, he's somewhat surprised to learn that he is suing Jack Kramer (the Chief Executive Officer of the nascent Association of Tennis Professionals), Donald Dell (the ATP's legal counsel and manager of Arthur Ashe and other players) and Commercial Union, an insurance company that sponsors the ILTF-sanctioned men's pro tour. Riordan, rebuffed just weeks earlier, is clearly trying a different tack, claiming that the subjects of the suit had used their influence in tennis to get Connors banned from the French Open. The suit was later dropped when Riordan's influence began to wane.

The news stories noted that Connors was actually suing his fellow players, almost all of whom were members of the ATP, and Ashe in particular (he was then president of the ATP), for $10 million. Connors would later claim to have confronted Riordan for taking this unilateral action that neither Jimbo nor Gloria knew about. But at the time, he issued no such disclaimer. In fact, he appeared to enjoy the notoriety.

In the years to come, Stan Smith would often wonder how different things might have been had he converted the match point he held against Ken Rosewall in the 1974 Wimbledon semi-final. A close friend of Arthur

Ashe and a former Wimbledon champ who was seeded no. 4 in the tournament, Smith lost a point-blank volley exchange at the net while leading by two sets to love and match-point up. It was a turning point. Thirty-nine-year-old Rosewall, without a single tournament win in the year for the first time in two decades, painstakingly reeled in Smith to win the match in five sets.

Up to that point, Smith was 4-4 against Connors. He was able to intimidate the twenty-one-year-old with a sledgehammer serve and his penchant for smothering opponents with net play. He makes Connors nervous, and both men know it. At 6ft 4in, Smith enjoys a tremendous advantage in reach. Having beaten Connors on the grass at Nottingham just a few weeks before Wimbledon, Smith feels confident. He's eager to exchange long-distance blows with the hellion who had spurned the overtures of Ashe, Cliff Drysdale and the other ATP members who tried to convince the maverick to join, or at least support, the official pro players' organization.

The ill feelings date back to 1973, when Connors was one of the very few top pros who failed to support the ATP's Wimbledon boycott. A Davis Cup stalwart, Smith was also disappointed by Jimbo's apparent lack of patriotic fervor for the event – a deficit that Connors has always denied having.

But at Wimbledon in 1974, where Smith is itching to get a crack at Connors and perhaps add a third Grand

Slam title to his collection, he manages to create the absolute worst outcome. Smith loses, and in stretching thirty-nine-year-old Rosewall to breaking point before capitulating, he tires and softens up the winner for a final against a player eighteen year his junior. Rosewall's nickname is 'Muscles', but it was originally bestowed upon him by an ironist.

Jimbo, however, has his own problems. Seeded no. 3, he meets Australia's Phil Dent in the second round. Dent is eager to exact revenge for the way Connors beat him in the final of Dent's own national championships. Since then, Connors reputation as a punk mama's boy has only grown, and resentment against him for refusing to join the ATP boycott of the previous year is still running high. He notices that when he walks into the locker room, every player turns his back. Ashe himself will write that every time he walks past Connors at Wimbledon he has an urge to smack him in the mouth — a most uncharacteristic reaction from Ashe.

Dent stretches the match to five sets. Deep into that final canto, Connors finds himself down 5-6, 0-30 — one stroke short of match point for Dent. But Connors wins the next point. Then, at 15-30, Jimbo hits a second serve so deep that both players assume it's a double fault — Dent's point. But the linesman never calls the ball out and Connors goes on to escape the game and win the match, 10-8 in the fifth.

Connors survives another five-set scare, this one from Jan Kodeš, in the quarter-finals. He is well into the tournament now, using the contempt his peers feel for him for emotional fuel. Jimbo's bigger problem may be the omnipresence of Chris Evert's dutiful mother Colette, who frequently travels with her daughter. Unlike Gloria Connors, who knows that, in Jimbo's words, 'boys will be boys', Colette tries to keep her love-struck daughter on a relatively tight leash. But her arms are practically torn from their sockets as she tries to keep track of Chrissie's comings and goings, all of them designed to secure a tryst with Jimbo.

Colette isn't all that sure that the Playboy Club of London is such a great place for her libidinous nineteen-year-old. Chrissie is, after all, from a good Catholic family. But loyal girlfriend that she is, Chris tags along as Jimbo and his pals – Năstase, John Lloyd (who would marry Chrissie in 1979) and Vitas Gerulaitis among them – gorge at the buffet and then retire upstairs to shoot craps or play blackjack.

Although there is no official record, it's almost certain that Connors runs into Ashe now and then at the club on Old Park Lane. For, while Ashe is a great temple-gazer and museum prowler (he immerses himself in foreign cultures with the sincerity and diligence you expect from a high school social studies teacher on a two-week vacation on the Continent), he's also magnetically attracted to the roulette wheel at the

Playboy Club. Were Ashe a different sort, he might even have backhanded Connors upon encountering him at the club, an incident that would undoubtedly have guaranteed both men enshrinement in the tabloid hall of fame.

Upon leaving the Playboy Club, Chrissie and Jimbo are routinely forced to run a gauntlet of paparazzi. They make jokes about knowing how it feels to be a Beatle. And they do a lot of what most young people in love most enjoy – so much so that Segura is concerned by how sluggishly Jimbo rolls downstairs for breakfast at the hotel in the morning. But Connors is young and fervid. He rolls through Dick Stockton in the semi-finals in four sets and is poised to take on Rosewall, the leathery-faced thirty-nine-year-old icon, in the final.

The following day, Saturday, Chris wins the women's event in a slaughter over the popular Russian Olga Morozova. The first half of what the Brits have dubbed the 'Love Double' is complete. The weather forecast for Sunday calls for temperature in the 90s (Fahrenheit), and Segura is concerned that Chrissie and Jimbo might be inclined to sneak away on Saturday night to celebrate her win. So he installs himself in Jimmy's room, where he will spend the night trying to sleep in a chair. At some point in the dead of night, Chrissie gently knocks on Jimbo's door. Segura opens it, sticks his head out and whispers, 'Jimmy still has to play. He needs his rest. After he beats Rosewall, you can have him on toast.'

It's possible that Chris immediately ran home and popped a few slices of bread into the toaster, preparing for the following day. For Rosewall is no match for Jimbo, and she knows it. He doesn't have the firepower to blow Jimmy away. He's nimble and mobile, but not explosively quick. Before every match during that Wimbledon, Segura had advised Connors to smack his service returns at the ankles of his opponents. As far as coaching advice goes, this is a little like telling a golfer he'll be just fine if he finds himself in a sand trap – all he needs to do then is hit the ball up on the green, preferably close to the pin.

Connors, though, is well equipped to carry out the plan. He has the finest service return in the game, and Rosewall's serve, while accurate, has relatively little pace. Given that grass-court tennis at this time is almost exclusively a serve-and-volley proposition at the time (even as Connors was the first in a new wave of all-court players), Jimbo simply buries Rosewall in a blizzard of aggressive service returns aimed at his shoe tops coupled with flat, powerful groundstrokes and stinging volleys. The score for Connors is 6-1, 6-1, 6-4.

If anyone still entertained doubts about the threat Connors presented to the pecking order, they are wiped away in London. Jimbo has clearly established himself as the best player in the world. The only remaining question is, 'Just how good is he?' Connors answers by duplicating his greatest feat, this time at the US Open, where he demolishes Rosewall by the even greater margin of 6-1, 6-0, 6-1.

Connors goes on to have, arguably, the most success-ful year in Open era tennis history. He wins fifteen events on a won-lost record of 93-6 (and two of those losses were by default due to injury!). Jimbo, Gloria, Segu and Riordan are flying high, higher than crows or sparrows or even vultures, almost as high as Icarus.

Ashe is 2-4 in 1974 tournament finals on the eve of the Wimbledon. It's a source of worry. He is also beginning to feel that the chemistry he once shared with Kathy, his girlfriend of nearly two years, has dissipated. Ashe is also the newly elected president of the ATP, an organization that still has a lot on its plate – as evidenced by the Wimbledon boycott of 1973. Furthermore, he can't very well wipe away his experiences in, and concern for, South Africa; the situation there is now a permanent part of his planning for the future, a part of his thinking and decision-making.

Then there there's Connors, an increasingly painful and disruptive thorn in the side of the struggling players' union and its new president. This irritation is exacerbated for Ashe by the fact that he can't seem to beat the *enfant terrible*. He senses an ominous truth in the accolades of a shell-shocked Tom Okker who, after losing to Connors in the semi-finals of Johannesburg in 1973 (thereby setting up the Ashe–Connors final), warned Ashe that Connors had played better against him than any other man, ever.

Coming from a highly ranked player who routinely bumped up against the likes of Rod Laver, Ken Rosewall, Ilie Năstase, Stan Smith and others, it was high praise – and a clear warning. Yet Connors' rivals look down their noses at him; some hold him in pure contempt. It was tempting for all of them, Ashe included, to retreat into a state of denial. Jimbo couldn't possibly be great; he's too much of a prick. Too much of a jerk. Too much of a mama's boy. We'll see if he's really got what it takes . . .

At the tournament in Nottingham, a Wimbledon tune-up where Ashe's pal Smith knocks off Connors, Ashe himself is beaten in the second round by Guillermo Vilas. Ashe is no longer quite so blasé about the threat represented by Connors, who has beaten him three times – and twice in barely over a year. But those matches were all on hard court. Ashe's game is well suited to grass, and he would like to show Connors that wicked slice serve and whiplash backhand on grass courts. Thanks to Vilas, he won't get that chance at Nottingham. The loss hurts, and Ashe can't see that deferring a first meeting with Connors on grass until a more significant occasion might turn out to be a good thing.

In the evening after losing to Vilas, Ashe works on developing the rules and guidelines that would ultimately become codified in the ATP rule book. He is also deeply immersed in the novels of Herman Hesse, which might turn out to be a bad thing. Complicated thinking, self-examination, even the very spell literature casts over the impressionable reader have never been touted as helpful to the athletic warrior.

When Ashe wakes up in the morning, he calmly informs his girlfriend Kathy that he's made the decision to break up. He says it with such chilling finality that she doesn't even bother to try talking him out of it. He just tells her he thinks they should 'call it off'.

Kathy immediately calls some friends in London, to ask if she can come to stay. Ashe offers to take her to the train station. He would have gladly drive her to London, but – there's still the doubles to play. Given that it's 110 miles or so from Nottingham to London, both Ashe and his girlfriend are entitled to feel deeply thankful that there's such a thing as doubles.

Ashe and his partner Roscoe Tanner lose in the doubles the following day. They move on to London, where Ashe loses to Tanner in the third round of Wimbledon. Connors is hurtling through the year, and Ashe is faltering. At the US Open, Ashe is dismissed in the quarter-finals by John Newcombe, sweeping away any chance Ashe might have had to meet Connors on the grass surface where Ashe is at his best. Ashe will not get past the quarter-finals in any tournament between the end of April and the end of September.

Back in South Africa for his final tournament of 1974, Ashe once again slashes his way to the final. And, once again, he is met there by Jimbo Connors, who picks apart his game 6-7, 6-3, 6-1.

It is nothing less than galling.

CHAPTER EIGHT

Caligula in Short Pants

'Jimmy Connors probably thinks he's the next best thing to 7-Up.'

Rod Laver

'The [hotel] suite was like a fight dressing room a half hour before the match. A tape recorder was blaring. Jimmy was bouncing up and down, screaming obscenities at the top of his lungs. Pancho Segura was sitting there like a fight trainer, yelling, "Keel him, Keel him."'

Bill Riordan, quoted in *World Tennis* magazine

East St Louis, Illinois, is in the icy grip of a harsh winter early in February of 1975, but Gloria Connors couldn't care less. She is with her Jimbo in Las Vegas, where he will play Rod 'the Rocket' Laver in a ballyhooed $100,000 winner-takes-all challenge match at the gambling mecca of Caesars Palace. The hotel-casino has even built a hangar-like stadium seating 4,000 just for the (presumably) one-off tennis match.

The unusual but undeniably alluring exhibition is the brainchild of Riordan, who claims that shortly after Jimbo walked off the court after savagely beating Ken Rosewall in the US Open final of 1974 he spat the words, 'Get me Laver!' That's Connors' version as well, because that comment Laver made about Connors and a certain refreshing carbonated beverage has stuck in Jimbo's craw. In fact, in Vegas he's had the slightly less than immortal words 'Better Than 7-Up' stitched on to the back of his warm-up jacket.

At this time Rocket Rod is generally regarded as the greatest player ever to swing a racquet. Only two men in the history of the game have completed a Grand Slam (triumph at all four Grand Slam events in the same year), Donald Budge and Laver. But Laver has done it twice – once as an amateur, once as a pro. Laver also won eleven Grand Slam titles despite being banned from the majors for some years after he turned pro, and a grand total of 200 titles in his exceptional career. He was rated the top player in the world by most authorities for seven consecutive years ending in 1970.

But Laver is thirty-six years old and semi-retired when Connors issues his challenge. The two have never played, partly because of the way the rival World Championship Tennis and Riordan's IPA tours were organized. At the few Grand Slam events both entered, one or the other has faltered before a potential meeting. Laver is somewhat past his prime, but still good enough to have beaten Arthur Ashe in the spring of 1974, the last time they played. He is a member of the old guard, and his attitude toward Connors appears to consists of a familiar mix of contempt, condescension and denial.

Still, how can a man who, before the advent of Open tennis, was often playing for a pittance – paid out under the table, no less – pass up a potential $100,000 payday (more than Connors earned for his 1974 US Open triumph), especially when it's been made clear that the loser of the 'winner-take-all' also would wind up making some $60,000?

The nationally televised match pits the owner of a Grand Slam against his notional successor. Connors did not accomplish a Grand Slam in 1974, but it may have been only because he was barred from the French Open. The cognoscenti have no doubt that, based on his performance in 1974, Connors probably would have joined Laver and Don Budge. The only qualifier is that playing to complete a rare Grand Slam in New York would have put Connors under an incredible amount of pressure at the US Open. But not many observers thought it likely that Connors would wilt – not at that stage of his career.

In any event, the 'heavyweight' challenge match captures the imagination of sports fans throughout the US, where there is just as much anti-Connors sentiment as support for the controversial champion. For such is his success that Connors' reputation is now that of a tyrant on the tennis court, a Caligula in short pants.

Connors likes to say he is trying to energize the game, and to help it shed its reputation as a sport for the well-heeled. But he is volubly accused of debasing and cheapening the sport. He rationalizes his vulgar antics as an attempt to entertain and excite fans, and to get the 'blue collar' element in society to embrace tennis. He seems oblivious to the fact that the typical taxi cab driver or plumber isn't necessarily dying to see athletes perform obscene gestures or throw boorish tantrums. They also have a notion of what is — and isn't — admirable and even 'classy', no matter what color their collars. And they know an exhibitionistic punk when they see one.

But Connors doesn't need to think about such things. He's winning — crushing everyone in his path. People are paying lots of money to come see him, and he's earning unheard of sums. He can — and does — wear a brand new pair of tennis shoes in every match without concern for the price for he gets them all for free. He broke off his engagement with America's sweetheart, Chris Evert, the previous September, partly because of both players' professional dedication. Now he has a house up in the Hollywood Hills, near his old buddies Dino Martin and Desi Arnaz Jr. 'Connors' is a name up in lights, in all the great capitals of the world. He can exert his influence and shape the game any way he wishes, because he dominates the playing field and he's also a box office attraction – as evidenced by this challenge match. Perhaps with all the surrounding publicity Jimbo mistakes being an object of interest with one of love.

Thus, on 2 February 1975, Connors feels entitled to jump around like a prizefighter on the side of the court as he glares, muttering, at Laver. Riordan, impersonating a corner man, lightly works over Connors' torso with his fists. The celebrities, including Clint Eastwood, Charlton Heston, Johnny Carson and popular Las Vegas comedienne Totie Fields, are filing in and taking their seats. Roy Emerson, Laver's coach, is ready; so is Connors' adviser, Pancho Segura.

Laver uncharacteristically delays his entrance – a nod, perhaps, to his own modest instinct for showmanship. When he finally walks on to the court there's an explosion of support and appreciation from the enthusiastic crowd. What's worse, for Jimbo, is that the crowd is actually booing him. 'I'm in Vegas,' he thinks, 'I'm in the USA. Really?' Connors can't quite see the relatively short (5ft 8in) Australian icon through the crowd, but when he notices that Eastwood, Heston and Carson are clearly participating in the lovefest for Laver he begins to dance around on the court, middle finger aloft, shrieking, 'Fuck you! Fuck you! Fuck you!'

Connors cannot fathom this outpouring of respect for the Rocket. It's an historic occasion, in his mind, the passing of the torch from one generation to the next. It's the wise, seasoned elder statesman against the brash but enthusiastic youngster — and in the younger man's domain, no less. Yet it seems clear that many of these people would like nothing more than to see Laver pulverize Connors. They view Connors with distaste, and that motivates the rebel. He plays savage, efficient tennis to win the first two sets. Segu is egging him on. Gloria Connors has a satisfied smirk on her face. Take that, Carson! Take that, Eastwood!

But Laver claws his way back and wins the third set. In the fourth, Connors closes in on the win, but Laver gamely staves off match points. Totie Fields, right in the front row, has been heckling Connors since the start of the match. As Laver fights for his competitive life, she keeps leaping out of her seat. She shrieks with delight when Laver wipes away yet another match point, whereupon Jimbo whirls around and gives her the middle finger salute, adding 'Shut up.'

There he is, then, the outsider come to wreak havoc and devastation upon all who would thwart his ambitions. He's a force of nature come to life, his progenitor looking on in a manner that can be described in any number of ways, none of them anything like 'motherly'. Gloria knows they dislike her son; she also knows he is whipping Laver and thus, by extension, them — all the thems, all the insiders, all those smug, ripe for ruination 'haves'. Allow Jimbo his 'fucks' and 'cocksuckers' and 'faggots' and don't say you didn't have his outrage coming.

It's hard to know what Gloria ever makes of the way her exhibitionistic son lewdly fondles his private parts; that's something she will take to the grave. Jimbo's gestures seem especially surprising because he is not known for being particularly exhibitionist in the locker room – where the boys often sit around buck naked, scratching here there and everywhere. He changes out of view. Yet time and again, under the glare of the floodlights in front of thousands, often including his own mother, he revels in such behaviour as stroking the handle of his racquet as if it were a penis.

Jimbo wins the match, 7-5 in the fourth set. Truly, he has no peer, and for his enemies the dark days are only just beginning.

While Connors is preoccupied gouging his pound of flesh out of Laver – and a mind-boggling payday out of the Heavyweight Challenge Match sponsors – the US Davis Cup team is in deep trouble down in Mexico. Raúl Ramirez upset Stan Smith in the first rubber, but Roscoe Tanner managed to secure a 1-1 tie in the second match. However, the Mexican pick-up team of Ramirez and Vicente Zarazúa stunned crack doubles players Bob Lutz and Dick Stockton, leaving Mexico on the verge of clinching at 2-1, on the final day.

At about the time Jimbo is finishing up with Laver, Mexico is well on its way to perhaps its greatest Davis

Cup triumph thanks to Ramirez's outstanding performance against Tanner in the fourth rubber. This is an unmitigated disaster for the US, even though Ramirez would eventually take his place on the list of 'best players never to win a Grand Slam event'.

The US won the Cup in 1972, defeating Romania, but Rocket Rod Laver and John Newcombe led Australia to a humiliating 5-0 whitewash of the defending champs in the final of 1973. Early in 1974, Colombia's two-man team of Ivan Molina and Jairo Velasco shocked the visiting US squad in zonal play. Just a year later, Mexico has taken a turn at whacking the red, white and blue *piñata*, inflicting another first-round humiliation on the most successful nation in the history of the competition.

That the US lost to Mexico while Jimmy Connors, the best player in the world, was hamming it up for the high rollers in Las Vegas is especially painful to the US tennis establishment. Critics lambaste Connors for turning a deaf ear to the call of national duty, but Jimbo doesn't see it that way and he doesn't give a hoot about what the critics say. He and Riordan are at war with anyone associated with the lords of tennis, or those who denied his chance at a Grand Slam in 1974. Besides, Connors' associations with Davis Cup are almost exclusively negative.

In his first (and only) Davis Cup appearance, in 1972, Connors felt like an outsider thrust into a cliquish nest of Donald Dell clients – starting with captain Dennis Ralston. To make matters worse, Connors' beloved grandmother, Two-Mom Thompson died during that tie, giving Jimbo a reason to quit the team and go home.

Next up in 1972 for Ralston's victorious squad was Mexico. The USLTA had a paid ticket waiting for Connors at the airport, but Jimbo never showed up, choosing instead to fly to London to practice on grass for Wimbledon.

Bill Riordan knows that the best defense is a good offense. When he is asked in Las Vegas to explain Connors' apathy, he lays the blame on his rival Donald Dell. Riordan claims that Dell controls the team, and uses it – and his players – as weapons in his war with Riordan and other independent operators. He accuses Dell of plotting to take over the game, like some latter-day robber baron of pro tennis.

Extreme as Riordan's accusations sound, he is by no means the only person who believes Dell is dangerously close to accumulating too much power – and inclined to use it liberally to improve his own position or leverage advantages for his clients. Cliff Drysdale, a South African who will eventually emigrate to the US, is every inch a company man. He is elected the first president of the budding Association of Tennis Professionals (on the nomination of Ashe). But he feels apprehensive about Dell and his army of talented, clean-cut, patriotic minions. They create an aura of elitism that somehow doesn't travel beyond the perimeter of their group. 'They were their own group, a clique,' Drysdale will tell me. 'It was an American thing, and very noticeable.'

Dell projects power and the potential for great conflicts of interest. He is not just the manager of the players, he is also the counsel to the ATP. He also moonlights as a television commentator, frequently calling matches involving a player he represents. It does not take Drysdale very long to decide that Dell's men are too easily led by him. Drysdale has no qualms about Dell's integrity, or his ability to serve the best interests of his players. But as an independent, he feels that Dell is collecting too much power in too many related areas.

Riordan likes to paint Dell and his 'co-conspirators' (chief among them Jack Kramer) as 'evil', and he revels in his newfound role as a mudslinger. He tells Curry Kirkpatrick of *Sports Illustrated*: 'The ATP stands for bans, boycotts and baloney. They are suing me for calling Kramer a piranha, which is nothing but a small fish. His ATP cronies get away with calling me a nihilist. Throughout history monopolists have labeled populists as nihilists while their leaders danced on the grave of Marie Antoinette.' Riordan likes that comparison, he tells Kirkpatrick bizarrely, 'Get that down, kid. That's an original.'

Riordan is as loose with his legal briefs as he is with his tongue, and the habit is catching. After Riordan files his $10 million lawsuit against the usual suspects for allegedly conspiring to keep Jimmy Connors out of the French Open, Kramer fires back with a $3 million lawsuit against Riordan and Connors, accusing them of libel. If Riordan has any regrets about accusing Kramer of 'lining his pockets', or characterizing Kramer and Dell as 'piranhas who have attempted to monopolize the game', he's keeping mum about them. He keeps firing away, and because he is the manager of the most riveting character – as well as the best player – in all of tennis, he takes full advantage of this bully pulpit. Both lawsuits were ultimately dropped, and came to nothing, partly because Riordan was let go by Connors.

Arthur Ashe himself becomes embroiled in this cross between soap opera and farce shortly after the US Davis Cup debacle in Mexico. Bitterly disappointed by the failure, and by Connors' unique status as the first great American player to spurn the chance to play Davis Cup, Ashe feels that he has found the younger man's Achilles heel in the quiet battle to either bring Jimbo into line or push him to the fringes of the mainstream. In print, he describes Connors as 'seemingly unpatriotic'.

Riordan does cartwheels when he reads that one, and he prepares to file what will be a $5 million lawsuit against Ashe. He knows just when to drop the bombshell as well. Just before the most important tournament of the year, Wimbledon.

*

Over the months following his challenge match win over Rod Laver, Connors abandons all restraint. He begins to call in all the chits created by his success, with plenty of help from other sybaritically inclined players, including the ever-present Ilie Năstase and Vitas Gerulaitis. Often, when Jimbo finds himself seated at a banquette in a night club, one hand wrapped around a drink, the other around the waist of an aspiring model or actress, he congratulates himself: 'Not bad for a working class kid from St Louis. Not bad at all.'

The Heavyweight Challenge Match concept is a winner. Riordan lines up John Newcombe for the next one, to take place just three months after the destruction of Laver. This time, the pot is richer yet; the winner will rake in $500,000 and the runner-up $300,000. Newcombe, who finished 1974 as the no. 2 player in the world behind Connors, has beaten Connors in the their two most recent meetings – one of them in the Australian Open final of 1974, played just a few months earlier.

Up to now, Gloria Connors and her late mother Two-Mom have gotten almost all the credit for Jimbo's development and game. Pancho Segura is seen by many as something less than the brilliant mastermind behind Connors' game. He's sometimes regarded more like an exotic minder whose colorful accent and blunt view of things are always worth a quotation or two (usually, it's something along the lines of: 'Jeem-bo, he is a keeler'). But at around the time of the challenge matches in Las

Vegas, the press finally begins to catch on to the enormous contribution of Pancho Segura.

The 'keeling' advice imparted to Connors before the Newcombe match? Segura believes that 'Newk' is not a good mover, so Jimbo needs to keep the ball low ('around his ankles'), and make liberal use of the low, skidding slice. Net result: Jimbo manhandles the popular, charismatic Aussie in four sets.

Not long thereafter, Connors is at dinner with a cousin of the pop singer and Las Vegas staple Paul Anka. Goaded by Riordan, Connors allows that he's a pretty good singer and has thought about pursuing a career in music after his playing days are over. In any event, he would like to cut a record. The cousin promises to introduce Connors to Anka. Astonishingly, a week later Anka meets with Connors and promises to write a few songs for him to record.

Connors' head is swimming on a daily basis. He's still practicing, but often in a groggy state from having rolled in at 5 a.m. He's drinking more than he should; he knows that. But so what? He's an Irishman. And he's still the best player in the world. When he tries to put his finger on what it feels like to be Jimmy Connors, the best he can come up with is that it's just like being a 'rock star'. The persona appears to represent some ultimate state of being to Connors.

Gloria and Two-Mom had warned him about falling into this trap, and his dissoluteness bothers him. Jimbo is, after all, a hard-working Midwestern boy who always listened to his mama. Now and then he is so stricken by guilt that Gloria's words are easily conjured: 'What you don't get accomplished by midnight probably won't get accomplished at all. There comes a time when you have to back off. The fun starts to go down and the trouble starts to go up.'

Wise words, he knows. But then there are some things that can only be accomplished, that you only want to accomplish, after midnight. And those are the things in which Connors is interested. Yet he plays — and wins — almost as much as ever. He endures a bout of glandular fever in early March, but he is 6-2 in eight finals as he makes his way to London in preparation for Wimbledon. His hedonistic tendencies, though, are not the only dangers he faces.

Over the past few months, Gloria Connors has become increasingly resentful of the credit Segura is receiving for the success of her son. Incredibly, though, Segura has never had his relationship with Jimmy and Gloria, or the details that govern it, formalized. And now he's being pulled every which way. Agents are coming to him with terrific offers that he feels obliged to take to Gloria, as if he were Jimbo's manager. But she has no interest in letting anyone but herself, with help from Riordan, manage her son.

Segu has always been deferential to Gloria on the coaching front. It's true that Jimbo claims that when his game is off, all it takes is a twenty-minute conversation with Gloria. But the reality is that her effective input ended the day she brought Jimmy to Segura. Yet she is leery of giving Segura too much credit. The coach is interested in a more businesslike arrangement going forward, but she sees no reason to get locked into anything. She already sees him as a threat; if Jimbo had Segu, why would he need her – the person who knows what's best for Jimbo?

Pancho's son Spencer, who has remained a close and loyal friend of Jimbo's, can tell trouble is in the offing. Back in the day, Two-Mom provided an effective, rational counterbalance to her obsessional and often unreasonably suspicious daughter. But that voice of reason has been silenced, and Jimmy himself simply lacks the guts to confront Gloria on the issue of Segura. Spencer knew that Gloria was becoming jealous of Segura, but there was nothing he or anyone else could do to stop it.

When Gloria and Segu begin to discuss the future, tension crackles in the air. At those times, Jimmy excuses himself to go practice. He never really knows how it came to be that he arrives in London in June 1974 without a coach. What he does know is that he's the defending champion, and still the best player in the world.

CHAPTER NINE

Into the Emerald City

'Ashe does not want to win badly enough. He does not devote enough time to tennis to realize his potential, does not think on the court, and chokes.'

Barry Lorge, tennis correspondent for the
Washington Post

Arthur [Ashe] didn't have the balls to confront me [about the Davis Cup]; instead he left a note in my locker at Wimbledon outlining his position. All he had to do was come up and talk to me face to face, man to man, but he chose not to. It annoyed me, but not so much as when he walked out on to [Wimbledon's] Centre Court wearing his Davis Cup jacket with USA emblazoned across his chest.'

Jimmy Connors

Charlie Pasarell is plagued by conflicting feelings in his room in London's Westbury Hotel. He's preparing to meet Arthur Ashe and their manager Donald Dell for dinner at the Playboy Club on the eve of the 1975 Wimbledon final. He's thrilled that Ashe, his former college roommate, has managed to slash and ace his way to his first Wimbledon final just a week before his thirty-second birthday. But Pasarell is anxious as well, for in the most resonant tennis match of the year, Ashe will have to face twenty-two-year-old sensation Jimmy Connors.

Among other things, Connors is presently suing Ashe for millions. Pasarell cannot for the life of him understand how or why anybody on earth would want to sue Arthur Ashe. He is as reasonable, thoughtful and conscientious a man as ever drew breath. But Connors has trained his audience to expect the unexpected. He comes to bury opponents, not to praise them.

Ashe is still winless in three matches against Jimbo Connors. In both of their previous meetings in sanctioned tournaments, Ashe managed to push Connors to the three-set distance. But Connors won both going away. The hellion has made a specialty of humiliating aging tennis celebrities, as Ken Rosewall and Rod Laver can attest, and now he seems to be restless again, eager to take his sledgehammer game to another potentially fragile icon. 'Well, if this match is going to happen, this is a good a time as any,' Pasarell tells himself. 'Arthur certainly is in with a shot.' His optimism, while faint, is not mere wishful thinking. Ashe has won six of eight finals leading to this meeting. Oddly, Connors has an identical record in 1975 finals.

Pasarell knows that over dinner the men will talk about what Ashe might do to beat Connors. *What am I going to tell him*, Charlie wonders? As he muses over his dilemma, his mind settles on that match in Los Angeles — when was it, '71 or '72? — where aging Pancho Gonzalez produced what Pasarell remembers as the greatest on-the-trot tennis lesson he's ever witnessed.

Of course, Connors was an energetic nineteen-year-old while Gonzalez himself was forty-three. It was unlikely that Pancho could keep up with Connors when the youth gave it the gas. Yet Gonzalez won that match, 3-6, 6-3, 6-3. And he didn't win it with his legendary cannonball serve, or powerful shots. Gonzalez dismantled Connors' deadly counter-punching game by refusing to play into his hands. Gonzalez had a wicked serve, but he kept the cannonball under wraps and hit many slice serves, denying Connors pace. The slice serves pulled Connors far off the court on the deuce side, and Gonzalez was able to step inside the court and play his next shot severely cross-court to Connors' weaker, forehand side.

Connors' own serve was so-so, and most players were tempted to go for a powerful, forcing return against him. But that also played right into Jimbo's hands, for it enabled him to feed on the pace created by an opponent. Gonzalez refrained from taking big cuts; he dinked and chipped and drop-shotted, drawing Connors in to the net. Then he would throw in a lob . . .

It was a masterful performance. Pasarell knows that one of Arthur's great strengths is his slice serve and, if necessary, he's capable of playing soft, almost spongy shots with a loose wrist. Now, if he can make his case convincingly, and Ashe can execute the plan . . .

Feeling better, Pasarell gathers up his wallet and keys and, with a spring in his step, leaves his room to go downstairs and meet Dell and Ashe for dinner, followed by a few rounds of blackjack and, of course, Ashe's favourite . . . roulette.

Ashe, an earnest student of cultures, is well aware of the Eastern concept of karma. Although it's more of a luxury than he can afford, he is entitled to feel that his karma at Wimbledon is generally good.

This event, which simply calls itself 'The Championships', takes place in the Emerald City of the tennis establishment. And Ashe, despite his activism on behalf of the budding professional class of players, is the ultimate tennis establishment man. It has been rewarding for him, but it has also caused him pain and anxiety. At Wimbledon, the men's singles draw is officially known as the 'Gentlemen's Singles', even if the tournament has always featured a fair sampling of rakes and bounders who are anything but. About Ashe, though, there is no doubt. He is a gentleman – very much an American, Southern gentleman, even if the color of his skin doesn't support the familiar stereotype.

When Open tennis arrived, many expected that Wimbledon would join all the other entities that were scrambling to redefine the way tennis is presented, based on the premise that the game was bursting out of its amateur era constraints. Rules mandating all-white clothing, polite silence during points, good sportsmanship – all such things were suddenly seen by some as out of step with the times, passé habits and affectations. Change was in the air, and it had agents aplenty – rude boys and rule-breakers, bad boys and individualists like Ilie Năstase and Jimmy Connors, who seemed to embody the ethos created in the tumultuous years following the 'cultural revolution' of the late 1960s.

But Wimbledon did not budge. The All England Lawn Tennis and Croquet Club's leadership had always operated on the assumption that what was good for Wimbledon was also good for tennis. From the very beginning, this has proved to be much more than an empty conceit or an exercise in self-justification. After all, in the early 1960s, with the game trembling on the brink of irrelevance, wasn't Wimbledon the Grand Slam event that unilaterally declared that it would embrace 'Open' tennis?

Perhaps the board members of the Wimbledon committee even discerned a counter-intuitive truth. The public that was busy creating the 'tennis boom' of the early 1970s was attracted to tennis not in spite of the game's aura of elitism, but because of it. The pendulum in society in the era of free love and 'do your own thing' egalitarianism may have swung toward license and sensation. But tennis easily penetrated that façade and exerted tremendous appeal to anyone who could be described as 'aspirational'. Wimbledon, with its associations of class and tradition, continued to represent a better life.

The more radical the changes elsewhere were, the more Wimbledon embraced the overarching theme that it was not just traditional and different, but timeless and better. It clearly was not subject to the whims and experiments demanded by commerce. Over time, Wimbledon began to look like the single fixed point in a rapidly changing world. The more entrepreneurs tried to 'popularize' the game — almost always watering it down in some way, and usually in order to line their pockets — the more appealing Wimbledon became.

As the years went on beyond the 1970s and well into the new century, the wisdom of the venerable club's leaders has been borne out in spades. But it's erroneous to assume, as some do, that Wimbledon hasn't changed. It has changed, profoundly in some ways, but never rashly, short-sightedly, or in the interest of cashing in on some new fad or public hunger. It has evolved slowly, much like one of Darwin's pet creatures. No element in the progress of the club has compromised the integrity of the tournament; it has a well-earned right to view itself as the standard-bearer for all of tennis.

In 1975, though, Jimmy Connors is not terribly interested in the integrity of Wimbledon or philosophical debates over the value of tradition. He has mixed feelings about the event, not least because it has not exactly enveloped him with open arms.

Before his first visit to Wimbledon, in 1972, Jimbo had heard all the usual stories. He was particularly juiced up by the prospect of being collected in front of his hotel for the trip to the club by a chauffeur-driven Rolls-Royce. But when he walked out of his hotel the morning of his debut, he was stunned to see nothing more than a typical black cab idling at the curb, waiting to take him to Wimbledon. Turns out the Rolls-Royce program had been discontinued the previous year.

Also in 1972, the British tabloids discovered Gloria Connors. During Jimbo's first match, against veteran Bob Hewitt, Gloria had called out encouragement to her son. The press took note of her enthusiasm and, having heard all about Gloria from their American colleagues, happily went about shaping and molding her into a suitably nightmarish creature, the 'Supermum' from hell.

The Wimbledon experience is turning out to be something other than all strawberries and cream for Jimbo, but he feels he can deal with it — just look at how efficiently he slaughtered Ken Rosewall in 1974. The tight-lipped disapproval written on the faces of the

Wimbledon committee members, the cold shoulders turned toward in the locker room by dues-paying ATP members, the titillating tabloid headlines that were simultaneously mocking and laudatory – he can put up with it all as long as he can go out there and demonstrate that he owns that soothing, lime-green rectangle that dominates Centre Court.

To Connors, Centre Court must seem old and decrepit, and it holds only about 12,000 people – less than a decent college basketball arena. The ivy looks like it's actually eating the exterior walls of Centre Court, it's so thick and clinging. There's that weird roof that hangs over half the seats, and the 'Royal Box' stuffed with women with frozen hair and stony-faced men who don't dare remove their suit or sports jackets no matter how oppressive the heat until the Duke of Kent does so. Taking the cue they all slip out of their jackets in unison.

But despite all that, Connors knows it's also true that you never have to wonder if the people in Centre Court are paying attention. You don't have that restless rumbling and buzzing background noise that suggests an inattentive audience. There are no idiots calling you out, 'You suck, Connors!' and nobody too important to ignore the basic rule of staying in your seat until the odd-game changeover. The people watching seem to really care. In that way, Wimbledon is okay.

*

Ashe's tournament begins without drama, with a tidy, four-set win over the very first man Connors ever played at Wimbledon, Bob Hewitt. A masterful doubles player, Hewitt is too slow and ponderous to do much damage in singles, but he has a good serve and excellent feel for the ball. Seeded no. 6, Ashe is happy to get through his first match.

Connors, the top-seed, rolls through the first round with even greater ease – demolishing Englishman John Lloyd with the loss of just six games in three sets. But during the match, Connors slips while chasing down a drop shot and hyperextends his knee. After he cools down, the pain in his knee is excruciating. When he wakes the following morning, his discomfort is even more intense. His knee is swollen and unable to support his weight.

Riordan arranges for Connors to be examined by a physiotherapist for Chelsea Football Club, who concludes that Connors has 'hairline fractures' in his shin (the condition is more formally known as 'anterior compartment syndrome'). Connors is assured that while his condition is painful it is treatable – mainly with rest. But rest is out of the question. After all, this is Wimbledon, not the Southwestern Bank and Trust Classic, played in northeastern Arizona. At the Grand Slam events, the players alternate days of play and days of rest; Connors has an entire free day to pursue therapy for his shin and knee.

In the second round, Ashe meets Jun Kamiwazumi, one of the very few Japanese players on the tour. Ashe gets a nice shot of confidence from his straight sets win, while Connors becomes embroiled in an interesting if never harrowing tug of war with India's rising star, Vijay Amritraj. In 1975, the Grand Slam events play a tie-breaker at eight-all in every set but the fifth and final one. That accounts for the exotic score by which Connors beats Amritraj: 9-8, 6-0, 8-6. Loath to show his opponents any sign of weakness, Connors refuses to wear any manner of support for his knee or shin. But he does avail himself of ultrasound, ice, massage, and the nuclear option, painkiller tablets.

Ashe's next victim is fellow American Brian Gottfried, a versatile, all-round player with a textbook slice backhand and sweet volley. Those are great assets on the low-bouncing, slick grass courts that characterize the first week of Wimbledon. But Gottfried doesn't have much with which to hurt an opponent, while Ashe has that heavy serve and whiplash backhand. The favorite overpowers his countryman in three sets.

Connors' opponent is British veteran Mark Cox, who in May 1968 became the very first amateur to beat a professional player (a feat made possible by the advent of Open tennis). Cox, a left-hander like Connors, defeated old pro Pancho Gonzalez at the tournament in Bournemouth, England. A Cambridge man and intelligent advocate for the ATP, Cox would attain a career-high ranking of no. 13. But at Wimbledon in 1975 he is no match for Connors, who trounces him, 6-4, 6-2, 6-2.

Ashe and Connors have completed the second major task at a Grand Slam event (after winning their respective first-round matches), surviving the first week. There is no play at all on the middle Sunday at Wimbledon, which only adds to feeling that the second week is an entirely different tournament, conducted after the winnowing process of week one. In both men's and women's events, the tournament is down to the final sixteen contenders. A few surprising faces almost always turn up in the last sixteen, but in 1975 none of them will survive to make the quarter-finals.

The assignment for Ashe is to dismiss Englishman Graham Stilwell, a versatile player who is cut out mostly for doubles. Inspired by the home crowd, Stilwell puts up surprisingly stiff resistance and manages to rebound from the loss of the first set to take the second. But Ashe settles in and wins the next two sets with little drama.

Connors has a far more dangerous opponent in the Australian attacking specialist Phil Dent. Connors shoots holes through Dent's defenses when the Australian serves and attacks the net — much as he did back in January 1974, when Connors defeated Dent in Australia to claim the first Grand Slam title of his career. On that occasion, Dent was able to win a set. This time, Dent gets a paltry five games — total.

Beyond the scores, though, not all is as well as it appears in Jimbo's world. There is the injury for one thing, although the way he's playing may lead one to wonder how much better he might be if he'd actually shattered his femur. Also during the second week, Connors is summoned before representatives of the Wimbledon committee to explain some comments he made to the press about the quality of the grass. It never occurred to Connors that the committee might be honestly curious to know what he was thinking, and why. In his autobiography he will claim to have made this speech when describing the meeting: 'This is bullshit and we all know what's going on here. Instead of worrying about the tennis, all you care about is what the press is saying about your precious grass. How about paying less attention to what I do off the court and more to what I do on it. Give me a break. And while you're at it, why don't you bring that bowler hat back to East St Louis and see how you get treated?'

Of course, it would have been unusual for any man at that moment to have been wearing a hat – bowler or otherwise – given that this interview was conducted indoors. Yet the formulation of the jibe is impressive in and of itself – at least it is when you consider that it's the brainchild of an ill-educated athlete who frequently brags that he's never read a book.

★

When it comes to a 128-draw Grand Slam event, the quarter-finals is the stage at which things become really serious. This time there have been no big holes opened up in the draw by a sensational upset. This time, the final eight men are all seeds, a fairly unusual occurrence back in the day when there were only sixteen seeds at Wimbledon. The final eight are a fetching blend of veteran champions and emerging stars: Connors (no. 1 seed), Ashe (no. 6), Björn Borg (no. 3), Guillermo Vilas (no. 4), Raúl Ramírez (no. 8), Roscoe Tanner (no. 11), Tom Okker (no. 9) and Tony Roche (no. 16).

Connors' next opponent is no. 8 seed Ramírez, a flashy, nimble Mexican who hits a heavy topspin forehand and wears his lustrous black hair in a Prince Valiant, much like Connors himself. While an outstanding doubles player, Ramírez is still a work in progress in singles. But he is already developing a reputation as a player who routinely rides herd on those ranked below him, but tends to shrink away when facing a superior player. Connors wins yet another one in straight sets.

Because he's seeded no. 6, Ashe is an underdog — at least on paper — in his quarter-final with no. 3 seed Björn Borg. The emerging Swedish star, who turned nineteen just days earlier, has a healthy respect for the explosive game of Ashe. Unlike Connors, the prince of the Riordan tour, Borg has been playing with the big boys on the World Championship Tennis circuit — and steadily taking his lumps. He's played Ashe twelve times already, and they're dead even with six wins apiece.

But this is 1975, and after losing the first set 2-6, Ashe gathers himself and takes the second, 6-4. The third set is a tension-filled, stomach-churning affair, but Ashe manages to emerge from the smoke with an 8-6 win. He finishes the job, 6-1 in the fourth.

Ashe is entitled to feel that he's being tested every which way at this Wimbledon, because his semi-final opponent will be Tony Roche, one of the most well-liked of all the legendary, old-school Australian champs. A five-time Grand Slam singles finalist, Roche was the French Open singles winner in 1966. A left-hander, he was also one of the great doubles players of his time. Roche won eight Grand Slam doubles titles – mostly with fellow countryman John Newcombe (Roche would also win an Australian Open doubles with Ashe, in 1976).

Because he's a lefty, Roche is good practice for Ashe in the event he meets Connors in the final. It turns out that Roche gives Ashe a more than adequate look at the chicanery of the southpaw. Although he is the lowest seed in the tournament, Roche takes the first set from Ashe, who rises to the challenge to win the next two. Then Roche rallies his tricky, slice-heavy game and manages to win the fourth set in a tie-breaker.

Ashe, however, remains cool. He knows that this may be his final chance to win Wimbledon; after all, Connors,

Borg and Vilas are all far younger – and already ranked higher. Ashe finally wins the semi-final with Roche, 6-4. Once again, that wicked serve has enabled him to hold with relative ease most of the time, and he's taken full advantage of his break-point chances.

Connors' semi-final opponent is Ashe's frequent doubles partner, Roscoe Tanner. A straw-haired, blue-eyed boy from Lookout Mountain, Tennessee, Tanner is yet another left-hander in a quarter-final round that features four of them. He is also the most dangerous one of them all when it comes to that formidable grass-court weapon, the serve.

Tanner has an extremely quick service action, married to a relatively low ball toss. The overall effect is something like a magic trick: one moment he's toeing the service notch and bouncing the ball, then, in the blink of an eye, that ball is in the air and – whap! – hit so hard and flat that it's barely visible to either spectator or the man waiting to return it. Tanner will be the Open-era service-speed record holder (with a delivery of 153mph) from 1978 until Andy Roddick smacks on at 155mph in a Davis Cup rubber in 2004.

Although Tanner is conspicuously slow-footed, he compensates with a surprising ability to slap sharp placements to end points. He knows that the longer the ball is in play, the less chance he has to win a given point. Thus, he tends to roll the die, intent on getting things over and done with quickly, one way or the other.

In this match, it is the other. Connors once again demonstrates why his service return is already hailed by most pundits as perhaps the best the game has ever produced. He puts unrelenting pressure on Tanner's serve, the kind of insistence that can rattle even the best server and force him to hit more second serves than he would like. And once the ball is in play, there's no contest at all. Connors can run circles around Tanner, and both men know it.

Tanner's real problem, though, is that he's unlikely to break Connors' serve. The serve is the weakest part of Jimbo's game, but the nature of the grass courts makes it more effective. That extra bit of help, combined with Tanner's so-so return, means that Tanner cannot take control of points, as Connors can, with his return. Even when he puts the ball back into play, he's at the mercy of Connors' punishing groundstrokes.

With such realities weighing on Tanner's shoulders, he is unable to avoid the occasional lapses that are so costly for a man who lives and dies by his serve. The failure to put a first serve in here, a volley error there, a double fault somewhere else – all of them are like rays of light falling through a door that is shut but by no means locked. Connors exploits those opportunities and builds on them. All he needs is one break per set, and he gets that – and more. He wins it, 6-4, 6-1, 6-4.

Connors will meet Arthur Ashe in a final for the fourth time, and he has every reason to believe that, once again, he will win. After all, he hasn't lost a set during this Wimbledon, despite the condition of his leg. And Ashe is bound to be a little leg-weary on Sunday, even with the day of rest, following his long, knockdown, dragged-out semi-final against Roche.

Connors, like most great players, has an ineradicable memory when it comes to real or imagined slights to his game. He had read after his last meeting with Ashe (in Johannesburg, 1974) that his rival suggested that a player could exploit Connors' serve, his forehand and his overhead smash. Jimbo got a kick out of that. After he won again in Jo'burg, bringing his 1974 take to fifteen titles, he was stimulated to gloat, 'With so many weaknesses, I sure won a lot.'

After his win over Tanner, Connors returns to Chelsea Hospital, where he once again meets with doctors. This time, their prognosis isn't very encouraging. They take Riordan aside and warn him that the damage to the leg is becoming dangerous. If Connors chooses to play the final, he may suffer a crippling, career-ending injury.

Riordan reveals the news to Connors, who dismisses the issue without so much as a second thought. Of course he's going to play, Connors tells Riordan. This is the Wimbledon final. He has to play. And nothing in the way he's been playing, despite all those painkillers he's been gobbling down, and all those exotic treatments, suggests that he cannot win this thing – perhaps even win it as handily as he's won his previous six matches. Perhaps thirty-one-year-old Ashe is ready to play Rosewall, or Laver, to Connors' Jimbo.

As Riordan turns to leave the room, Connors stops him. 'Bill,' he warns. 'Don't tell Mom.'

Riordan pauses, not sure what he can say to reassure Jimbo. As always, he tries to make light of the situation. 'Don't worry, kid, you're strong enough, you're young enough, and you're good enough. You'll be fine. I'm not worried.'

Riordan eventually drops Connors off at their hotel and excuses himself to go off and run some errands. Years later, Connors will allege that one of Riordan's 'errands' was a quick trip to a bookmaker, where the manager places an enormous bet on the Wimbledon final, in which Connors will be a 11-2 favorite.

Riordan bets on Ashe.

After dinner at the Playboy Club, Ashe, Charlie Pasarell and Donald Dell return to the Westbury Hotel to relax and strategize a bit before turning in. All of them are thinking similar things. Earlier in the day, Ashe had taken a call from US Davis Cup captain Dennis Ralston, yet another friend and Dell client who is mortified by Connors and his attitudes and antics.

Ralston, a Wimbledon finalist in 1966, advised Ashe to play to Connors' forehand, keeping the ball low. 'He isn't good at those balls,' Ralston said. 'He makes a lot of errors when he has to hit up on a low ball, compared to waist-high balls. He doesn't miss many waist-high balls.'

Ashe lays this out, and his companions nod and agree with the assessment. Pasarell then spells out in detail how Pancho Gonzalez mastered Connors in that unforgettable match of 1971. For all the power of his famous serve, Gonzalez was no ball basher. Once the ball was in play, Gonzalez had a wonderful toolbox to draw upon, ranging from gently struck slice backhands and sharply cut volleys to an assortment of dinks, chips and drop shots. His catlike quickness enabled him to outmaneuver and outfox opponents.

Pasarell was convinced that Gonzalez's blueprint remained valid, for Connors' game had improved but not really changed in the four-year interim. Pasarell knew Ashe was intelligent and skilled enough to embrace it. If he could cling to his strategy and make it work in the face of Connors' barrage of flat, stinging groundstrokes, it would also give the underdog a psychological advantage.

Ashe and company decide that he would plug away at Connors' backhand return. He would feed Connors relatively slow balls, right down the center of the court, preferably forcing him to hit low forehands.

The other addition is a tactic with which Ashe has already experimented, albeit with mixed results. He will dust off the most seldom used weapon in his arsenal, the lob.

Connors closes on the net aggressively, thus he's vulnerable to the lob — especially the relatively low trajectory lob. Also, at 5ft 10, Connors is relatively short. His reach, especially on the backhand side (where he is hampered by his two-handed grip even on the backhand smash), is limited.

That this is the first meeting of the men on grass courts just might work out to be an enormous advantage for Ashe. The properties of the surface seem favorable to his strategy and tactics. But it will take enormous skill, as well as nerve, to pull off the upset. Should Ashe play with anything less than precision, or dip his brush into the wrong color on his palette at any given moment, he will surely get the ball shoved right down his throat. He will be this year's Ken Rosewall. Spectators might walk away muttering and shaking their heads, 'What was wrong with Ashe? He didn't even look like he was trying. Connors killed him.'

The four man 'brains trust' (including Ralston) has come up with a game plan that makes Ashe feel that all bets are off — despite his three previous losses to Connors, despite his 11-2 underdog status. It's a plan that even that brilliant lone wolf Pancho Segura might be hard put to match. But Segura won't even get a chance to match wits with Ashe's coterie. He's been driven off by jealous Gloria Connors, and Jimbo is left twisting in the wind.

Proud, brash and confident, he doesn't even know it.

.

It is the day of reckoning: Sunday, 5 July.

Connors did not practice at all on Saturday, the day of the women's Wimbledon singles final. He was resting his leg. Now, on Sunday morning, he is warming up on a court in Wimbledon's hinterlands, a court where they usually play junior matches. But the early arrivals at Wimbledon are among the most determined and knowledgeable of fans. They know Connors and Ashe will be out there, somewhere, having their pre-match warm-ups. These usually consists of a fairly light hit, and if the fans are lucky they might get to see their idols goofing around, hitting trick shots and trying to stay loose.

Connors does not disappoint. He is put through his paces by his pal Ilie Năstase. It's hard to tell if it's because Connors wants to protect his injured leg, or maybe he feels extremely confident, but he's in a particularly chipper mood. Perhaps it's that, across the net, the gifted mimic Năstase is doing a hilarious imitation of Ashe – from his service motion right down to the way he walks. And the fans gathered around the court are loving it.

Ashe will warm up later, right before the final. In fact, part of his game plan is to go out to play the match while still sufficiently exercised to perspire. Ashe believes it's imperative for him to get a quick start, to get Connors off-balance, and early. It will help if he's already elastic and warm.

Ashe recruites Ray Ruffels to warm him up, partly because, like Connors, Ruffels is a lefty. Just as important, though, at least from a karmic point of view, Ruffels has already had the honor of warming up two previous Wimbledon finalists — both of whom went on to become the champion. Of course, Ashe is a rational man. But even a rational man can see that warming up with Ruffels certainly can't hurt.

Ruffels is somewhat puzzled during their spirited warm-up. At one point, as he collects balls at the net, he asks Ashe, 'I can't understand this, Artie. You're always lobbing today. But everybody knows you never use the lob.'

Ashe smiles at the question and offers some obtuse explanation without going into great detail.

CHAPTER TEN

Worlds in Collision

'I've never seen Arthur [Ashe] really discipline himself. He plays the game with the lackadaisical, haphazard mannerisms of a liberal . . . Nobody in his right mind, really, would try those little dink shots he tries as often as he does. When he hits out, he just slaps. He plays to shoot his wad. He hits the ball so hard that it's an outright winner or he misses the shot. When he misses, he just shrugs his shoulders.'

Clark Graebner, describing his Davis Cup team-mate and rival Arthur Ashe, in John McPhee's book *Levels of the Game*

'I'm trying, for Chrissakes, I'm trying!'

Jimmy Connors, in response to a fan urging him to 'come on' during the 1975 Wimbledon final

Down in the lobby of the Westbury Hotel, waiting for Arthur Ashe on the morning of the Wimbledon final, Donald Dell has an idea. He finds a piece of hotel stationery and writes down three things for his friend to remember: *keep the ball low, and mostly on Connors' forehand side; serve him wide to the backhand; use the lob.*

When Dell really wants to get Ashe's undivided attention, he always calls him 'lieutenant'. Before Ashe disappears into the bowels of Centre Court to prepare for the match, Dell calls out, 'Lieutenant.' He hands Ashe the note. 'Good luck.'

A grand total of 338,000 spectators have trooped through the turnstiles at Wimbledon during the 1975 tournament, establishing a new record. Perhaps the luckiest of them all are assembled for the men's final — the first between Americans in a full twenty-nine years. Many of them understand that they may be about to witness yet another passing of the torch into the eager hands of Jimmy Connors. The young American's international celebrity is at a peak; in late April he made the cover of *Time* magazine back in the US, a privilege rarely bestowed upon an athlete, along with the headline, 'Storming the Courts'. But there is no sign of overwhelming, pro-Connors sentiment in this crowd. And that can be attributed to the popularity of Arthur Ashe. No black man has ever been champion at Wimbledon, and if you were to create an appropriate one to achieve that honor you might come up with someone like Ashe. The contrast he embodies with Connors is inescapable and manifest on almost every level, and that accounts for some of the palpable tension in the air, which is otherwise soft and still. The temperature is ideal, and the overcast skies absorb the sunlight and redistributes it softly and evenly. Neither man will have trouble picking a lob out of the sun on this day.

During the preliminaries, Jimmy Connors appears loose and confident. Squinty-eyed, he grins at the photographers who record the coin toss, and fires off some wisecrack. He glances covertly at the player guest box, which is across Centre Court from the chair umpire, to his right, and just above one of the two main scoreboards. Gloria sits there, flanked by Bill Riordan on the right and — presumably in place of exiled coach Pancho Segura — British actress Susan George. The box is shared by the special guests of the finalists, the Connors contingent on the right side, Ashe's supporters on the left. Alongside Connors, Arthur Ashe stands with his brow furrowed, as if he's trying to remember a telephone number, or perhaps he's wondering where he's seen that stunning woman sitting next to Gloria Connors. He bites his lip.

The men are ready. The crowd is fidgety, a few of the patrons as close to the court as the first row of seats along the side line nervously puff on cigarettes. Their anxiety may be explained by the fact that for the first time in Wimbledon history, bookmakers are allowed in the grounds. Fans who attend Wimbledon are generally a conservative lot, but there are a fair number of oversized collars, lively print shirts with the three top buttons open, leather jackets and belled sleeves on display.

Having won the toss, Connors elects to serve first. He accepts two balls and stands at the baseline. As the umpire intones, 'Connors to serve. Quiet please', the noise subsides. Jimbo looks down at his shoes, leisurely bouncing a ball. He's like a schoolteacher, waiting for the children to settle down before beginning class.

'Play.'

Connors is still in no hurry. He lifts his head, looks up at the gallery as he basks in this moment, and smiles knowingly. He appears a man in full control of his destiny, perhaps even smug. It's a surprisingly cavalier attitude, but one to which Connors might feel entitled given his history with Ashe.

But, then, this is not just a new day, this is their first meeting on grass courts. Ashe believes that the uneven nature of grass courts makes it difficult to get 'grooved' on them, and that the unpredictable bounces can be especially frustrating for a player who, like Connors, relies on precision and consistency. There are advantages, Ashe knows, to playing the kind of 'dinks' and 'slapdash' tennis that his former Davis Cup team-mate and pal Graebner once described so dismissively. The turf court appears 'fast', but it's only because the ball skids on the grass and remains relatively low because turf is both slick and absorbent. Dinks and drop shots sit down nicely on it.

Connors tosses the ball for his first serve. It flies down the center line, Ashe moves to hit the backhand, but the ball is upon him before he can get a good swing and it caroms off the frame of his Head Competition racquet.

Game on.

Set 1

Gloria Connors and Two-Mom are famous for having taught their boy how to play what is often described as a 'woman's game', made lethal by the strength, quickness and timing not so much of a man but of a particular man – Jimbo. The women emphasized consistency, smooth and compact stroke production and mobility over the more common search for power in men's tennis. It was not a difficult path to choose. Women traditionally regarded the serve less as a potential weapon (for lack of power) than as an unavoidable way to put the ball into play.

Of course, it took a certain kind of excellent athlete to break the mold as succesfully as Connors did. The reality is that Jimbo has unique talents, and Connors' mothers chipped away like the proverbial sculptor liberating the figure trapped inside the stone – flaws and all. The flaws in Jimbo's case, include his inability to exploit some of the natural advantages of being left-handed. The left-hander's slice and kick serves are deadly in the left-side service box, where they can pull a right-hander far off the court. For a somewhat mysterious reason, the wide serve of the right-hander never seems quite as effective in the deuce court – even against a left-hander. Connors, though, lacks both the sound mechanics and the power to hit wicked lefty slice serves or aces.

Technique-wise, the Connors serve looks a mess. Great serves are born of abandonment; the server, his back arched, his knees deeply bent, his face turned to the sun, launches himself at the ball like a salmon attempting to leap an impossible cascade. Connors, by contrast, seems to want to protect the ball. He lines up, bending forward at the waist, holding the racquet and ball together. He draws them back toward his body and shifts his weight rearward, on to his back, left heel as he makes his toss. Instead of exploding up and out toward the ball, he appears to want to smother it. His body, seen in a side view when he serves, forms a letter 'C'.

This conservative service tries to mask and minimize the disadvantage in Connors' inability to generate adequate serve power. It enables Connors to consistently put first serves into play, and he relies on them to keep opponents honest, unable to feast on his even less menacing second serves. Unlike Ashe, master of the 'cannonball' flat serve, Connors rarely hits flat. He likes to use topspin (brushing the strings over the top of the ball) or slice (striking the ball high on the outside) because spin forces the ball to move in more of an arc and it loses energy faster – and thus drops into the service box more readily.

Connors holds the first game with ease, Ashe feeling his way with caution.

Preparing to serve his first game, Ashe strides to the baseline ramrod straight, like the good soldier that he is. He is tense, though; it's evident in the way he forcefully bounces the ball on the turf with the face of his sleek, silver Head Ashe Competition racquet parallel to the turf, like a child playing patty-cake. Ashe lines up and takes a long look down the court, at Connors.

Ashe begins his service motion with an exaggerated takeback, sweeping his racquet back behind him like a man preparing to fling a bowling ball. It's an uncharacteristically flamboyant gesture for a man as conservative as Ashe, but quickly rescinded as Ashe brings the racquet back in front of himself, leans forward and gently touches the butt of the racquet atop the ball. This is the signal to begin his toss. He arches his back as he sweeps the racquet back, allowing the head to drop behind his back.

The Ashe service motion is fluid, and quicker than most. His arm is long and limber allowing him to generate good racquet speed. The result is a serve that is more like the sting of an asp than the bite of a lion. Ashe considers himself one of seven men on the tour who are capable of putting 40 or 50 per cent of their biggest serves into play and have fewer than 20 per cent returned. He describes the serve as 'the most personal thing' in tennis, and while he rightly considers his own one of the best, he also feels it's a bit 'light'. In Ashe's opinion, the best serve belongs to John Newcombe. It's slower, but players describe it as 'heavy'. Ashe feels that the quick, light cannonball at which he excels can be timed by a good returner. And Connors is already being hailed as the greatest returner in the game.

So Ashe decides he will stay away from the temptations of the ace-making cannonball. He can afford to give it up, for his slice is no run-of-the-mill second-serve shot. You can see that by the somewhat cramped way he hits it, raking the strings over the upper, outside edge of the ball, arm remaining close to his body. This gives the ball heavy spin; on slippery grass it skids and 'bends' much like a well-struck free-kick in football. Ashe holds his first service game with ease.

The score is 1-1, Connors serving at 40-15. He directs a serve with a fair amount of spin toward Ashe's backhand. Ready, the returner hits up and over the ball. For a flash, it is uncertain that the return will clear the net. Connors hesitates. As a result, his routine backhand volley smacks the white net tape and falls back on his own side: 40-30.

Ashe fields Connors' next serve with a heavily sliced backhand return. Connors responds with a backhand aimed to Ashe's forehand. Ashe slaps at it in a way that might inspire Clark Graebner to leap from the sofa, exclaiming, 'See! See! That's exactly what I mean!'

The ball travels slowly well inside the side lines and sits down low on the bounce thanks to underspin.

Connors can do little with it, so he shovels it into the air, hoping to lob over Ashe. But Ashe leaps and drives the ball deep to Connors' forehand corner. Connors makes a game effort to reach the ball but barely gets a racquet on it.

Deuce.

Ashe returns the next serve crisply, to Connors' forehand. Connors pulls the trigger on a cross-court forehand, but Ashe nimbly covers the court and responds with a heavily sliced backhand down the line. Connors rushes to the ball, but fails to get enough lift with his backhand dig. He drives the ball into the net.

Advantage, Ashe.

Facing break point, Connors misses his first serve. Ashe takes the second serve with a sliced backhand, cross-court. Connors hits a probing forehand deep – but not deep enough – to Ashe's forehand side. Nonetheless, he charges to the net and Ashe tosses up an excellent lob that drives Connors back. Going for broke, Connors hits a smash right down the center of the court, forcing Ashe to hop out of way. The ball appears to land out, but the linesman remains mum.

Ashe looks at the official, puzzled. He turns to chair umpire George Armstrong. Ashe's 'protest', while mute and hardly worth the description, is unusual. Dr Johnson might have frowned upon this gesture. But times have changed. And the crowd is clearly on the side of Ashe. Numerous spectators protest, giving voice to Ashe's complaint, calling that the Connors smash was out. This is a blow to Jimbo. He is, after all, the defending champion. He is the youthful ruler of all he surveys. In his mind, Ashe may well be just another over-thirty stand-in for Rosewall. Why would the crowd want him to win?

A new, temporary rule at Wimbledon allows line judges to 'defer' to the umpire in the event of a dispute over a line call. The linesman avails himself of the opportunity. Armstrong chides the crowd with those familiar words 'Quiet, please'. A moment later he repeats himself, with stentorian emphasis. Pausing for effect, Armstrong finally explains that the linesman has elected to defer. Armstrong awards the point to Ashe.

Game, Ashe.

Although it's just the third game of the match, it contains all the themes that will unfold. Connors put five of eight first serves into play in the game, but Ashe was able to return them the way he wanted. Recalling Segura's advice, Jimbo tries to keep the ball on Ashe's forehand side. But the Ashe forehand held up; it even did damage. When Connors failed to get the error on that wing, he aimed for the backhand – where Ashe hurt him with heavy slice. Connors was unable to batter away, forcing Ashe back off the baseline. He was unable to control the points because Ashe was both quick to attack and provided Connors with very little to work with in the way of pace and angles. Ashe has provided a preview of all his strategic tools, including the one-two combination that earned him the final point of that game and the first break of the match: a short ball to the forehand, luring his aggressive opponent into the net, followed by a deep lob. It's a good omen. Up in the player guest box, Dell takes a deep breath and exhales.

But breaking serve is just the front end of the job. If a player fails to consolidate the break with a hold, the momentum shifts back. Ashe appears to be on his way to doing just that in the next game, serving at 2-1. Failing to put his first serve into play, Ashe can only watch as Connors fires a forehand bullet past him, down the line, off a second serve. Jimbo follows with another screaming forehand pass off Ashe's first volley. He is off the leash now, but Ashe remains unruffled. He reels off the next few points, ending the critical game with a drop shot.

Connors is rattled now. Serving at 1-3, he loses the first three points through sloppy play. At break point – a virtual set point – Ashe takes advantage of Connors' aggression again. As Jimbo rushes the net, Ashe prepares to hit a backhand; at the last moment, he angles the face of the racquet and gently lifts a lob over Connors' backhand shoulder. Madly scrambling back to his baseline, Connors can do nothing but take a desperate swipe at the ball. Game, Ashe.

The crowd greets the accomplishment with an enthusiastic salvo. Instead of the anticipated ritual slaughter they are likely to see a competitive match today. The combination of Ashe's underdog status, his racial identity and his bearing, have the crowd in thrall. But it's early in the match; it would be foolish to read too much into one set.

With a two-break, 4-1 lead, Ashe holds and then breaks Connors yet again to take the set, 6-1. Sitting in his chair at the end of the set, Ashe removes a piece of paper from his racquet cover. It is the note from Dell. Ashe studies it for a moment, then folds and replaces it. Up in the gallery, Dell watches, stunned. And delighted.

Set 2

Ashe holds the first game of the second set. Connors wins the first point of his ensuing service game, but it's a brief respite from his troubles. The ensuing points play out like a nightmare. Connors drills a forehand into the net off an Ashe backhand return. He gets sucked into the mid-court by a soft shot and jerks the backhand approach shot long. Ashe blocks back his next serve to present Connors with a challenging half-volley that he mangles.

15-40.

Connors puts his next serve into play and recklessly charges the net. The pace of the return catches him by surprise; he's still on the run as he stretches to his right and the ball caroms off the strings of that explosive steel racquet. It is an uncharacteristic loss of control by a superb athlete, and clearly a sign of his growing frustration.

Ashe to serve, at 2-0.

It's still too early for Connors to be fully aware or overly concerned about this deadly combination of Ashe's superior level and devastating strategy. It is too early to panic, besides which Connors is not the panicking kind. He knows that, thus far, Ashe is in the place known as 'the zone'. Phlegmatic even at the best of times, Ashe isn't merely exercising self-control on this nerve-wracking occasion. Something else is going on; there's an aura of serenity around Ashe, confidence so natural and profound that it doesn't call attention to itself in the form of gestures or body language.

Ashe is in the zone, and in the zone time slows down and that little yellow tennis ball looks the size of a beach ball. A player in the zone can do no wrong, but the zone opens – and closes – unpredictably. Connors is thinking that Ashe can't possibly continue at this level, not for an entire match. Jimbo will bide his time, ready to take full advantage when the inevitable decline occurs.

However, he doesn't really factor in the strategy of Ashe. Although he was taught a lesson along similar lines many years ago by Pancho Gonzalez, it is nowhere near the front of his mind. He was a raw youth then, and in the past year and a half nobody, but nobody, has been able to devise a strategy that hurts Connors. There is no such thing as kryptonite on Planet Jimbo.

Ashe has been pounding relentlessly at Connors' weaker, forehand wing. The errors Connors produces highlight the disadvantages of Excalibur, the T-2000 racquet with which Connors so frequently misfires. It is hard to control at the best of times, thanks to the inherent properties of the chromed steel frame combined with the 'trampoline' stringing system. Connors has marvelous eye-hand coordination; he's the last pro standing in the battle to control the power of the frame. But it still isn't a forgiving racquet and on this day Connors needs much forgiving.

The men playing this final aren't aware of it, but they are pointing the way to the future of the game in a number of ways, starting with their equipment. Ashe's own Head racquet is as novel as his rival's. The Head Arthur Ashe Competition is often compared to a canoe paddle or a snowshoe because of its shape. If anything the visual effect is even more futuristic than that created by the T-2000. The Head Comp is a sandwich composed of fiberglass between two panels of aluminum. Most wood racquets are pleasantly rounded at the edges; the edges of the Head Comp are right angles.

Ashe's racquet is less explosive than the T-2000, but more easily controlled – and more conducive to making the dinks and chips with which Ashe so liberally sprinkles his power game. Unlike Connors, Ashe doesn't need any extra help on his serve. Despite its radical appearance, the Head Comp plays unlike any of the new aluminum or steel racquets flooding the market. In fact, it plays mostly like the wooden racquets that the new wonder frames are rapidly replacing.

Serving at 2-0, Ashe suddenly abandons a key tactic and delivers three consecutive serves to the lethal Connors backhand. None of them are returned. Ashe goes back to the forehand, but hits a double fault. He returns to the backhand at 40-15, taking full advantage of the way his slice swerves out of the court, and of Connors' limited reach with that two-handed backhand. Ashe wins the game, 3-0.

Connors wins the first two points of his ensuing service game but his game again stalls. When he loses the next point, a disgruntled male spectator shouts, 'Come on, Connors!'

Without missing a beat, Connors spits back, 'I'm trying, for Chrissakes, I'm trying!'

'Well,' legendary BBC announcer Dan Maskell offers. 'I've never heard *that* before on Centre Court.'

It is, of course, a mild rebuke, but Maskell leaves it at that. Ashe rewards him with yet another swift hold of serve. He's perilously close to winning the second set, and after yet another service break in the sixth game he closes it out just as he did the first, 6-1.

Ashe recognizes that something incredible is happening on Centre Court. So does the crowd. The applause with which they greet the end of the set is heartfelt, but also somewhat tentative, as if the spectators are not quite sure what they are seeing. Is this really how things will play out? Ashe asks himself the same question as he sits on the changeover before the third and perhaps final set. His eyes are closed. It looks as if he is meditating. The thought he has drifts through his mind slowly, like a cloud on a sunny, still day. Usually, a player gets into the zone in Fort Worth or Bologna, he thinks. But who knows? It sure feels like he is in the zone at perhaps the most important moment of his entire career. Can it last?

Set 3

Connors and Ashe both have murderous backhands, but they are different and disparately employed. Connors likes to use his flat backhand as a pile-driving rally tool, or to bang out spectacular passing shots. He has a short, simple takeback and a compact swing, which partly account for his prowess as a returner. Occasionally, he will slice the ball, especially on an approach shot, but that's awkward for a two-hander.

Ashe has one of the most glorious flat backhands in the game, although it's too long and elaborate a stroke to be helpful returning serve. He uses it mostly to hit winners from anywhere on the court, or to pass. When he does trot out his backhand, it is truly a thing of beauty. At the moment of impact, Ashe appears to be driven back by recoil, as if he'd just fired a heavy caliber rifle. He can end points from anywhere on the court when he detonates that backhand, yet the sum effect is fluid and graceful. But he has kept that punishing shot under wraps, relying instead on his natural affinity for slice.

The forehand is the relative weakness in the games of both men, more glaringly so on this day for Connors. Ashe freely admits that the forehand volley is his Achilles heel, yet he has muffed but one of those thus far. And much to his delight, Ashe has noticed that Connors' tendency to hit bullets works in his favor when it comes to net play with the forehand. All he needs to do is stick his racquet out with the face angled for the direction he wants the volley to go and the pace of Connors' attempted pass takes care of the rest.

However, both the dodgy forehand and that brilliant backhand let Ashe down at a crucial moment in the match. At the beginning of the third set, Ashe makes inroads in yet another Connors service game. Should he win the game, the match could become the kind of debacle with which Connors is all too familiar. But this time he will be on the wrong end of the score, and somewhere in Sydney, Australia, Ken Rosewall will lean back in his chair and exclaim, 'Yes, there is a God!'

Ashe has two break points at 15-40, but he dumps a soft forehand into the net to waste his first chance, and pulls the trigger on a big backhand that flies out to return the score to deuce. Connors almost pitches over on to his face as he ducks Ashe's wild backhand, an indication of how surprised he is when Ashe finally attempts his signature shot.

Connors manages a hold for 1-0.

Thus far, Connors has done nothing but struggle and

Ashe has dominated, experiencing nothing like the letdown that sometimes follows right on a period of excellent play. Even as he lets Connors off the hook in the first game, Ashe remains inside that cocoon of serenity. But both men know that a player cannot predict when he suddenly leaves the zone any more than he can predict when he enters it. And a missed opportunity of the kind Ashe just experienced is sometimes enough to break the spell.

Ashe's game shows no signs of erosion, though. He holds easily, after which Connors also takes care of his service game. It's the first time in the match that Jimbo has produced consecutive holds. Ashe also holds, for 2-2.

In the fifth game, though, Connors again falls behind 0-40 — mostly through egregious errors. His game is like the engine of an old car on a cold morning. It coughs, turns over, appears to run — and dies again. Connors eliminates one break point, but on the second Ashe drills one of those memorable backhands right at Connors' midriff. The ball appears to be hit hard enough to drill a hole in Connors' belly but, leaping back, he drops his racquet low to fend off the ball and avoid the humiliation of being hit. His serve is broken, he trails, 2-3.

On the changeover, Ashe still looks utterly relaxed and oddly divorced from the proceedings. The crowd seems almost mesmerized. There is very little of the familiar white noise as spectators chat or unwrap sandwiches or open bags of chips. The atmosphere is subdued.

Ashe is sitting almost back-to-back with Connors behind the umpire's chair, which only heightens the contrast between the two men. Connors sits furiously chewing gum and massaging the leather grip of his T-2000 with a green towel. He wipes his nose in the towel, takes a quick look to see if he unearthed anything, then runs the towel through his hair. He gets up from his chair and heads for the court. The swagger is gone now. He just walks, no longer dropping wisecracks or making eye contact with the spectators. He's immersed in his predicament. Ashe, who has not had his service broken all day, need only hold serve three more times to win the match.

Connors begins the game by ripping a backhand service return winner past Ashe. He wins the next point as well, but then Ashe briskly takes it to thirty-all. Ashe wins the next point, but Connors takes it to deuce. Ashe hits a second serve to the backhand and moves forward. But he hesitates for a split second as Connors strikes; Ashe is unsure if he will take the ball in the air or just as it bounces. The moment of indecision causes Ashe to fumble an awkward backhand half-volley. It's the first sign of confusion from Ashe in the entire match. Connors wins the game with an excellent backhand lob hit on the run. Ashe, leaping and stretching to full height, gets the ball only with the top of his frame and hits it long.

Three-all. Jimbo is still alive. Riordan hikes shoulders and whispers a few encouraging words to Gloria, whose expression remains stony. Riordan laughs, but his jocularity appears forced. Having the members of the rival camps occupy the same guest box is a vestige of easier, earlier times, when the competitors were friendly. If Dell so desired, he could easily reach over, grab Riordan by the collar and pommel him. But precisely because of their proximity, both men are on their best behavior – even though the hair on the back of their necks must be standing on end.

Connors struggles mightily – again – to hold the next game, only to see Ashe hold his serve with relative ease. Although Connors cannot maintain an acceptable level of play, he has clawed and kicked his way back into contention. He manages an easier hold to take a 5-4 lead, yet Ashe refuses to crumble. Two holds later, Ashe is serving to stay in the set at 5-6. A light, soft drizzle – little more than a mist – envelopes Centre Court, adding a somber touch to the progress of the set.

Ashe, though, is feeling no anxiety as he serves to extend the set. The men haggle and fight the score to thirty-all. From there, Connors snaps out a service return with such velocity that Ashe, approaching the net, doesn't even have time to bend to play the half-volley. Connors has set point, and he claims it with a dazzling forehand passing shot. He celebrates with a yell and a fist pump; he is Jimbo again, and it feels pretty damned good.

Set 4

Ashe sits in his chair on the changeover after Connors takes the third set, staring out into space. At his age and with his disposition, he knows that sometimes he is his own worst enemy. He tends to over-analyze his results, especially losses. He feels he ought to have won more often at the major events. These are things that Ashe, a thoughtful man, sometimes broods over, and they are the things that can ruin a player if he allows his mind to begin weighing and sifting them in the course of a match.

Ashe is no fool. He knows as well as anyone else in Centre Court, as well as his friend Donald Dell, or Charlie Pasarell, who is back at home by now, anxiously glued to the television, that he might still lose this match. He is, after all, streaky Arthur Ashe. Unpredictable Arthur Ashe. He's so dispassionate that some wonder if he still has the gumption to rise to an occasion. He's a popular, wealthy, highly respected figure. Does he really even enjoy competition any more, never mind crave it in the manner of, say, Jimmy Connors?

Ashe is aware of all that, but he is thinking about something entirely different, and in a somewhat unusual way. Like an observer floating on a cloud high above the Centre Court, Ashe tells himself, 'It's about time he got hot. This is to be expected.' Ashe also knows that Connors was so far behind in the match midway through the third set that the pressure was off. That freed up his wrist and loosened his spirits. It's easy to play great when you're really far ahead – or really far behind.

In fact, Connors' fightback is almost comforting to Ashe, for the idea of Jimbo rolling over and folding in three swift sets challenges Ashe's concept of reality. Ashe knows he still has work to do, and he isn't distressed by that – not at all. He has not felt anxious for one moment in this match. He knows that now the pressure will be on Connors again, for now the defending champ is back in it.

All that is well and good while Ashe is sitting in his chair, but the reality of his situation comes knocking quickly enough on the court. Connors manages to hold the first game of the fourth set, and he tears through the next game, the killing shot yet another backhand service winner down the line. Jimbo punctuates the winner with a guttural shout. He adds another hold to lead, 3-0.

The crowd appreciates his effort, showering him with applause. The trance Ashe created with his brilliant play and detached manner is broken. Connors is making a match of it, and by gosh that merits respect. The shift in momentum can be read in the way the crowd seems more relaxed, more willing to give a little here, a little there, now to one man, now to the other. If Ashe can't manage to win this Wimbledon after such a start, Connors will deserve all the praise heaped upon him. In the guest box, Donald Dell feels hollow. He has seen this kind of movie before; there is a sickening inevitability to the way some of these remarkable comebacks play out. And wouldn't it be just like this vulgar, self-absorbed punk Jimbo Connors to emerge from this match not admonished but bathed in glory? It is too early to think about that, but Dell knows that down 0-3, Ashe has no room left for error. If Connors rolls through the set, it's likely that Ashe's poise and confidence will be shattered – not that you'd be able to read any of that in his demeanor.

Ashe stabilizes in the ensuing game. He builds a 40-15 lead and wins it with a gratifying forehand volley winner, hit from well below the net cord level. Sweet. He's on the board at 1-3 and, even better, he then breaks Connors with a running forehand passing shot that Connors cannot return. A prolonged volley of applause rolls down over Centre Court. Ashe feels himself back on track, and proves it with an authoritative hold in the next game.

It is three-all.

Much as Ashe suspected, Connors' game begins to fray at the edges now that the match is close again. Jimbo struggles through a hold, and Ashe glides through one for four-all. He is subtly stepping up the game, relying on his more conventional, powerful weapons. Instead of the soft chips and dinks and slices, he's now cracking his serve and hitting freely with his backhand. He's emboldened, sensing both the chance and need to finish Connors. Ashe's instincts tell him he must reach out and seize the match, instead of hoping Connors will continue to misfire and lose it.

Umpire Armstrong calls for new balls to start the ninth game of the set. This is good for Jimbo, for the new balls add a bit of snap to his serve, at least until each is whacked a few times. Sure enough, Ashe mishandles a backhand return to give Connors the first point. Ashe has trouble with the next serve as well. Connors steps out of the way and lets the ball drop – only to see it fall good for fifteen-all. Ashe takes the next serve with his backhand and makes a terrific return, low to the Connors backhand volley. But Jimbo digs it out and returns again to the backhand.

This time Ashe loads up and, dancing back out of the way as he swings, he fires a backhand bullet down the backhand line. Many years later, this kind of shot will come to be called an 'inside-in' backhand, and it is one of the most difficult of all shots to hit. The typical stroke travels cross-court; it is both the easiest and safest of shots. The 'inside-out' shot that Rafael Nadal and others will make so popular goes cross-court – but on the same side of the player's body where the stroke originated. The inside-in travels the same way, but it is hit from close to the side line. It's like threading a needle, and hitting it demands great body control because it is the least natural shot in the arsenal.

A volley error by Connors brings about break point at 15-40. The next serve targets Ashe's backhand – again. The returner is ready; he rolls over the ball with a full swing, ensuring that it drops below the height of the net before it reaches Connors' service line. The ball lands so quickly that Connors can only try to spear it like a fish. The ball bounces high in the air and over the net, where Ashe, onrushing, takes a huge cut with his backhand. But by the time he makes contact Connors has his back turned, heading for his chair. He knows he's broken. The match is now on Ashe's racquet.

The first serve of the final game is a wicked slice that Connors, pulled well wide of the deuce court, barely touches. The last serve of the final game, with Ashe leading 40-15, is a carbon copy. Connors manages to get his racquet on the ball and loft a return but Ashe, at the net, bats it away with a gentle pat as applause shatters the stillness.

Ashe whirls toward Dell up in the guest box and salutes him with a raised arm and clenched fist. Some will mistake this gesture for the controversial Black Power salute, but this is not a win for Black Power, or any other kind of power. It is not a win for 'the good guys', nor one for the honor of those poor Aussies made to appear like lumbering old dinosaurs on the verge of extinction at the hands of Connors, an uncouth Cro-Magnon with a gleaming steel spear.

This is a win for the tennis player Arthur Ashe, a man swaddled in doubts at the height of his career. It comes at a time when too many people feel they have a stake in him, when legions are telling him who he should be, what he should think, whom he should represent, and how. Those people all tend to forget that Ashe is not just a symbol and a spokesperson, he's also a tennis player. Until just a few moments ago, he was a tennis player who felt that despite all the accolades, money and fame he still had something to prove to himself. He felt that something exquisite and wondrous that had always been within his reach eluded him. He wouldn't think of or call it 'greatness', but that is just what it was.

Understanding that at a visceral level, he will soon write of this moment: 'It was not foremost about beating Jimmy Connors. The primary thing is that I won Wimbledon.'

But still . . . Ashe drops his racquet by his chair while the applause continues to roll down on to the court. He picks his blue warm-up jacket off the chair and proceeds to zip it up, the letters 'USA' emblazoned on the left breast, covering his heart. It has been a long and unpredictable road to this moment – never more so than in the past three hours of his life.

Epilogue

'It was a destiny richly deserved, a triumph that spread happiness and satisfaction throughout the world of tennis because it had turned a good man into a great champion.'

Journalist Richard Evans, writing in *World Tennis* magazine,
on the 1975 Wimbledon final

The 1975 Wimbledon final isn't on the short list of great Wimbledon finals; it was too one-sided to qualify for that. But it is high on the list of great achievements at Wimbledon, and among the most resonant of upsets. It also remains perhaps the most vivid example of a win created by an intelligent strategy. Lest we forget, though, strategy is nothing without execution. In the end it was Ashe's ability to transform the thought into the act that made this such an exceptional final. Would that we could all manage that transformation in any number of areas.

The other great distinction of this match was the way it helped usher in a new era. In that regard, it was somewhat deceptive. For the sake of verisimilitude, Connors ought to have won it. In the light of future events, Ashe's win can be regarded as a final, thunderous salvo fired on behalf of the old guard and the values it represented. Ashe is the last American Grand Slam singles champions who earned his college degree. He was the last to serve in the Armed Forces. He subscribed to the code of gentlemanly conduct, represented his country with pride and dignity, and took an active role in the affairs of his profession – to the benefit of his colleagues and peers. He also sought to become a true citizen of the world, taking full advantage of the opportunities the touring life afforded to experience other cultures.

All successful professionals must put tennis first, there's no getting around the mandate to assign the game the top priority in life – at least until family comes along. In Ashe's time, it was still possible to control the demands of the profession and reconcile it with a more or less 'regular' life. But within one generation (assuming that a generation in tennis is comprised of roughly ten years) a player who would qualify as great would be controlled by his profession. Starting with Connors, gifted players would increasingly exist in something of a gilded cage, richly compensated and widely known, but in thrall for better or worse to the profession.

Values and mores certainly change over time; sometimes it's a pendular process. Just as Ashe et al. ultimately gave way to Connors and McEnroe, those men were succeeded by the likes of Pete Sampras and Roger Federer, both disciplined gentlemen and good sports more in the mold of Ashe than of Connors. Yet even they would not have the breadth of interests, knowledge and social engagement that characterized Ashe. Among other things, the obligations of their profession ruled out such explorations. The Open era has been extremely generous to the stars of tennis, but it has demanded much of them, too.

Soon after the 1975 Wimbledon final, Jimmy Connors dropped his libel lawsuit against Arthur Ashe. Like Riordan's other lawsuit, against Dell and Kramer, this one was dropped with no resolution. The instigator of the suit, Connors' manager Bill Riordan, said of the Wimbledon debacle, 'My credibility was damaged when he [Jimmy Connors] got out of shape and started skipping tournaments. He took a cavalier attitude toward me. It's a mother problem.' Connors ditched Riordan by the end of the year.

Clearing up the paperwork after their separation, Connors' accountants discovered that Riordan had returned a significant portion of Jimbo's 'Heavyweight Challenge' earnings to the host, Caesars Palace – to pay off the gambling debts Riordan had accumulated at the hotel. In May 1976, less than a year after he sued Ashe on behalf of Connors, Riordan filed a new lawsuit against Connors alleging breach of contract.

Arthur Ashe went on to win three more titles in 1975, but as defending champion in 1976 he took a fourth-round loss to up-and-coming youngster Vitas Gerulaitis. Ashe would not win another Grand Slam singles title, and stumbled in the first round at Wimbledon the final two years he played, 1978 and 1979. However, he did partner with Tony Roche to win the Wimbledon doubles in 1976.

Jimmy Connors continued his rampage after he lost the Wimbledon final, but his year ended on a down note: he was soundly beaten by Raúl Ramírez in the fifth and decisive rubber of the USA vs Mexico Davis Cup tie. Connors made the finals in six of his final seven tournaments, but won the same number as Ashe – three. He was upset at the US Open, then played on green Har-Tru clay, by clay expert Manuel Orantes.

The week after he won Wimbledon, Ashe took a meeting called by an international group of activists seeking to persuade the ILTF to bar South Africa from competing in the Davis Cup tournament of nations. The push was successful, but partly through Ashe's influence individual players who were not officially representing South Africa were allowed to travel and compete freely.

Two weeks after the US Open Connors appeared on a new TV show, *Saturday Night Live with Howard Cosell*, to sing 'Girl, You Turn Me On', a song written for him by his accompanist on the piano, Paul Anka. Shortly before he went on stage, Connors would claim, his surprisingly supportive patron Anka presented Jimbo with a contract.

Loyal to Connors despite the way Jimbo had just stood by and allowed Gloria to push Pancho Segura out of the picture, first-year law student Spencer Segura read the contract on the spot. Alarmed, he forbade his friend to sign it. Extremely nervous, Connors appeared on stage with enormous, black perspiration stains on his light-colored shirt and gave a performance that was painful to behold.

In early 1977, Ashe married artistic photographer Jeanne Moutoussamy while wearing a cast on one foot due to surgery for a heel spur. Because of his recuperation, in the ensuing months Ashe's ranking fell all the way to no. 257. He then mounted a comeback that lifted him up to no. 14 in the world at the age of thirty-five.

In June 1976, Swedish sensation Björn Borg, then barely twenty, suddenly developed a little extra pop on his serve. It was the final piece to fall into place. Borg would go on to win Wimbledon five times in succession starting in '76. From the start of 1977, Borg would accumulate a 14-2 record against Connors.

In July 1978, Connors lost the Wimbledon final to Borg. In the six Grand Slam tournaments following his loss to Ashe at Wimbledon in 1975, Connors won only once. When *Sports Illustrated* writer Frank Deford raised the issue, Connors defiantly declared: 'They'll be talking about '74 when I'm dead . . . Don't forget what I did in '74. Nobody can ever take '74 from me.'

In July 1979, Ashe suffered a heart attack while conducting a tennis clinic in New York. In December, he underwent quadruple bypass surgery. He planned a comeback to tennis, but while on a family vacation to

Egypt a few months later he experienced a second heart attack. He returned to New York.

In the fall of 1979, Jimmy Connors married Playboy model Patti McGuire. Although McGuire all but prostrated herself before Gloria, Jimbo's mother resented her deeply and barely spoke a word to her until her death at age 82 in 2007.

In April 1980 Ashe announced his retirement from tennis. Upon leaving the game behind, Ashe dedicated himself to writing and social activism, advising a number of large companies on, among other things, race relations.

In the summer of 1980, Jimmy and Patti had a son, Brett. They would later have a daughter, Aubree.

In 1983, Ashe underwent a second bout of heart surgery in order to correct an issue left over from his original bypass.

In 1983, Donald Dell, Ashe's agent, great friend and confidant, signed Jimmy Connors as a client. Under Dell's management, Connors earned bushels of money and won what would be the last of his eight Grand Slam titles at the US Open in 1983. It was his fifth US title. At the end of that year of resurgence, Connors admitted to his wife Patti that he had been unfaithful to her and demanded a divorce. But the couple eventually repaired their relationship.

In 1986, Arthur and Jeanne Moutoussamy Ashe adopted a daughter, Camera — named for her mother's occupation.

In 1988, after working with a team of researchers for nearly six years, Ashe published a three-volume book, *A*

Hard Road to Glory: A History of the African-American Athlete.
He remarked that the book was more important to him
than any tennis title.

In September of that same year, Ashe was hospitalized
again – this time after experiencing paralysis in his right
arm. He was diagnosed as HIV positive, most likely from
a blood transfusion he received during his second heart
surgery. Arthur and Jeanne tried to keep his condition a
secret, in order to protect the privacy of their family.
They were successful for about four years.

Also in 1988, Connors auditioned for a role as host of
the daytime version of the popular game show, *Wheel of
Fortune* ('My wife and I never miss an episode,' he said of
the show). But he didn't get the job and Merv Griffin,
creator of the show, refused to release the tape of
Connors' audition, saying, 'It wouldn't be fair to Jimmy.'

Connors burned both ends of the competitive candle
through most of the 1980s, playing high-quality
tournament tennis as well as numerous exhibitions.
One demonstration nearly caused an international
incident. While playing an exhibition against Andrés
Gómez in Ecuador, Jimbo repeatedly grabbed his crotch
and cursed. Connors was finally warned that the
president of Ecuador was present; if Jimbo continued to
play with himself he would be arrested and jailed.

In the thirteen Grand Slam events Connors played
between 1985 and the end of 1989 (by which time he was
thirty-seven) he reached five semi-finals and three

quarter-finals. He remained in the top ten through that entire period, although he ended up with a career-losing record against each of his three great rivals: Björn Borg, John McEnroe and Ivan Lendl.

In March 1989, Arthur Ashe Jr's father Arthur died of a stroke.

In 1990, Jimbo stunned sports fans worldwide with a riveting performance at the US Open. Thirty-nine years old by the end of his run, Connors made it all the way to the semi-finals in Louis Armstrong Stadium at the USTA National Tennis Center in Flushing Meadows — hamming it up all the way for the crowd.

Connors continued to earn a fortune with the help of Dell, and he would need it. He had a persistent, growing gambling problem, and in 1991 he learned that his brother John, who helped Gloria manage Jimmy's accounts, had been stealing large sums of his money.

On 8 April 1992, editors at the newspaper *USA Today* informed Ashe that they were going to reveal that he had AIDS. The Ashes pre-empted the newspaper by calling a hastily arranged news conference where Ashe, forcing back tears at times, divulged his condition.

In February 1993, just a week before he died of AIDS-related pneumonia, Ashe published his final book, a memoir entitled *Days of Grace*. In it, he wrote: 'Quite often, people who mean well will inquire of me whether I ever ask myself, in the face of my diseases, "Why me?" I never do. If I ask "Why me?" as I am assaulted by heart disease and AIDS, I must ask "Why me?" about my blessings, and question my right to enjoy them. The morning after I won Wimbledon in 1975 I should have asked, "Why me?"'

In April 1996, Connors played his last match on the main pro tour: a three-set loss in Atlanta to fellow American Richey Reneberg. All told, Connors amassed 109 titles in sanctioned events. He won 1,253 official matches during his career – a record unlikely ever to be broken.

In August 1997, the USTA dedicated the brand new centerpiece of its National Tennis Center (home of the US Open), Arthur Ashe Stadium. Regarding the stadium on one occasion, Connors was rumored to have turned to a companion and said, 'I win the sonuvabitch five times and they name the stadium after *him*?'

In May 2014, Connors published his autobiography, *The Outsider*.

Arthur Ashe was laid to rest in Richmond, Virginia, as per his long-standing request, alongside the mother he barely knew but deeply loved, Mattie Ashe.

Jimmy and Patti Connors live on a ranch near Santa Barbara. Neither of their two children took to tennis, but Jimbo does a little coaching now and then.

Acknowledgements

Given the number of years I have in tennis, it would be impossible to thank everyone who helped shape my relationships with, and opinions about, Arthur Ashe and Jimmy Connors. I knew and sometimes worked closely with most of the principals in this book, so I will limit my acknowledgements to those among the living who had a direct, shaping influence on this book.

Donald Dell, who managed Connors after Ashe retired and has a place on the short list of people who had a seminal influence on the Open era, was an invaluable source. So was Charles Pasarell, who remains one of the most well-liked men in the game. Spencer Segura is a realist, but also a perceptive observer and independent thinker - as his spectacular post-tennis success attests. Stan Smith, ever the model citizen-player, was generous with his time, as were those old WCT hands, Cliff Drysdale and Fred Stolle. My colleague Joel Drucker helped me out periodically, and photographer Art Seitz was there when I needed him. I must single out both Doug Smith's wonderful book, *Whirlwind*, for the fascinating material Smith unearthed on the evolution of tennis in the African-American community and Caroline Seebohm's comprehensive biography of Pancho Segura. Jeanne Moutoussamy Ashe was both encouraging and helpful.

On the publishing side, I am delighted - and lucky - to be represented by Byrd Leavell and Scott Waxman at the literary agency that bears their name. At Aurum, Lucy Warburton was a patient and kind editor from start to finish, and Richard Collins did an outstanding job with the copy-editing.

Bibliography

Ashe, Arthur, with Frank Deford, *Portrait in Motion*, Boston: Houghton-Mifflin, 1975.

Ashe, Arthur, with Arnold Rampersad, *Days of Grace*, New York: Knopf, 1993.

Baltzell, Digby, *Sporting Gentlemen: Men's Tennis from the Age of Honor to the Cult of the Superstar,* New York: Free Press, 1995.

Bodo, Peter, *The Courts of Babylon: Tales of Greed and Glory in the Harsh New World of Professional Tennis*, New York: Macmillan, 1995.

Connors, Jimmy, *The Outsider: A Memoir,* New York: Harper, 2013.

Drucker, Joel, *Jimmy Connors Saved My Life*, Toronto: Sport Media Publishing, 2004.

McPhee, John, *Levels of the Game,* New York: Farrar, Straus & Giroux, 1969.

Smith, Doug, *Whirlwind: The Godfather of Black Tennis.* Washington D.C. , 2004.

Seebohm, Caroline, *Little Pancho: The Life of Tennis Legend Pancho Segura*, Lincoln, Neb.: University of Nebraska Press, 2009.